The *New* American Sampler Cookbook

The *New* American Sampler Cookbook

Edited by

Linda Bauer

The Kent State University Press
Kent, Ohio, and London, England

© 1991 by The Kent State University Press
All rights reserved
Library of Congress Catalog Card Number 90-47480
ISBN 0-87338-435-0
Manufactured in the United States of America

Illustrations by Aaron Sutherland.

Library of Congress Cataloging-in-Publication Data

The New American sampler cookbook / edited by Linda Bauer.
     p.   cm.
   Includes indexes.
   ISBN 0-87338-435-0 (alk. paper) ∞
   1. Cookery, American.   I. Bauer, Linda.
  TX715.N5116   1990
641.5′0973—dc20   90-47480

British Library Cataloging-in-Publication data are available.

To Michael and Christopher, the lights of my life.
May you never know hunger, but never forget
those who do.

CONTENTS

ACKNOWLEDGMENTS

Special thanks to President and Mrs. Bush, Vice President and Mrs. Quayle, and members of Congress and their families for their generous contributions to this collection. The late Senator Spark Matsunaga, with customary compassion, shared several recipes in support of this project. Thanks also to my family for eating some odd combinations of dishes, and to my husband for his patience while teaching me to use the computer. I also thank the staff at the Kent State University Press who feel that fighting world hunger is a worthy cause. And to the supporters of World Vision, may this book help to feed many hungry people and relieve their burden.

INTRODUCTION

Several years ago I collected the favorite recipes of members of Congress and the president and vice president and put them into *The American Sampler Cookbook,* an effort born out of the dream of fighting and someday defeating famine. With the success of the cookbook, I decided that I would do a second collection only if I could find a charity dedicated to helping the plight of the hungry and meeting their needs, a charity to whom proceeds from the book would go and be wisely used.

Over the next few years, while considering a sequel and searching for a charity, a few coincidental meetings with friends—old and new—were influential in my discovery and choice of World Vision, a respected international Christian relief and development agency involved in the fight against world hunger. Two friends who work abroad as missionary and teacher, and who are familiar with international relief organizations, highly recommended World Vision, as did Rosemary Trible, wife of Virginia's former senator. A chance meeting with football great Rosey Grier led to a long conversation about my project and his enthusiastic recommendation of World Vision.

The inspiration and encouragement I gained from these people and many others and my excitement over having another opportunity to fulfill my dream have all worked to produce *The New American Sampler Cookbook.* Enjoy!

Appetizers

Pâtés

Dips

Hors d'oeuvres

First Courses

SHRIMP PÂTÉ

Representative **John Dingell**—*Michigan*

12 ounces canned shrimp, drained
½ cup butter, softened
1 cup mayonnaise
1 tablespoon horseradish

Chop shrimp and mix in remaining ingredients.
Chill for several hours. Serve with melba toast or
favorite crackers.

Makes 24 servings.

PICNIC PÂTÉ

Senator **Christopher Bond**—*Missouri*

Mushrooms are the magic in this savory pâté. Tuck it away in a picnic basket along with a hefty supply of sandwiches, pickles, and fresh fruit, and enjoy an outing under the Gateway Arch.

4 **tablespoons butter**
½ **pound fresh mushrooms**
4 **green onions, minced**
4 **tablespoons sherry**
8 **ounces liverwurst**
2 **8-ounce packages cream cheese, softened**
1 **teaspoon chopped fresh dill**
1 **teaspoon chopped fresh chervil**
2 **teaspoons Dijon mustard**
  salt and freshly ground pepper to taste

Melt butter in a skillet. Sauté mushrooms and green onions until soft. Stir in sherry, cool. Place mushroom mixture and remaining ingredients in a food processor or blender, process until very smooth. Transfer to a crock or serving bowl. Refrigerate for at least 24 hours before serving. Garnish with sprigs of fresh dill. Serve with party rye and a selection of pickles.

Makes 12 servings.

SHRIMP DIP

Senator **David Durenberger**—*Minnesota*

- 2 **4½-ounce cans shrimp**
- 8 **ounces cream cheese**
- ¼ **pound melted butter**
- 2 **tablespoons lemon juice**
     dash Worcestershire sauce
     grated onions to taste
- ¼ **cup mayonnaise**

Blend ingredients together and refrigerate overnight. Serve on crackers. Will keep for long periods when refrigerated.

Makes 12 servings.

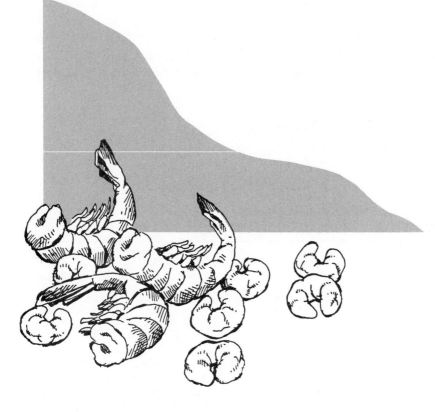

IDAHO APPLE DIP

Senator **Steve Symms**—*Idaho*

6 Idaho Red Delicious or Rome apples
   lemon juice
8 ounces cream cheese
3 tablespoons heavy cream
4 ounces bleu cheese, crumbled

Cut cored, unpeeled apples into bite-size chunks.
Insert toothpicks into apple chunks and dip in lemon
juice. Insert other ends of toothpicks in a whole
apple. Blend softened cream cheese with heavy
cream. Add bleu cheese. Serve with apples as a dip.

Dip variations:
1. Serve with pineapple cheese spread blended with
dairy sour cream.
2. Blend pimento cheese spread with a little
mayonnaise.

Makes 12 servings.

EASTER EGG DIP

Senator **Christopher Bond**—*Missouri*

Reviving an old tradition, we hosted our first Easter-egg hunt at the Missouri Governor's Mansion on the lawn in 1973. Since our son Sam arrived, the hunt has become an annual event. This unusual dip proved the perfect solution for leftover Easter eggs.

2 tablespoons lemon juice
1 tablespoon onion juice
1 teaspoon coarse ground mustard
2 teaspoons mustard
½ cup mayonnaise
½ teaspoon Tabasco sauce
½ teaspoon seasoned salt
6 hard-cooked eggs, chopped
¼ teaspoon white pepper
4 ounces olive-and-pimento cream cheese, whipped
fresh parsley or dill, chopped

In a mixer or blender, combine juices, mustards, mayonnaise, and Tabasco sauce. Add eggs one by one, beating after each addition until smooth and light. Beat in salt, pepper, and cream cheese. Turn into chilled bowl, smooth top, and garnish with chopped, fresh parsley or dill. Serve with raw vegetables or assorted crackers. May be spread on bread for tea sandwiches.

Makes 2 cups.

CURRY CAPER DIP

Senator **Christopher Bond**—*Missouri*

My favorite dip for raw vegetables always recalls memories of the good friend who parted with this gem.

1 cup mayonnaise
½ cup sour cream
1 teaspoon crushed herbs, such as basil, thyme, and oregano
¼ teaspoon salt
⅛ teaspoon curry
1 tablespoon onion, grated
1 tablespoon fresh parsley, chopped
1½ teaspoons lemon juice
2 teaspoons capers, drained
½ teaspoon Worcestershire sauce

Mix all ingredients. Chill. Serve with crudités. For a colorful presentation, spoon the dip into a hollowed-out red cabbage or eggplant.

Makes 1½ cups.

PICADILLO DIP

Representative **Steve Bartlett**—*Texas*

This recipe may also be used with flour tortillas. Because it freezes so well, it is easier to make in big batches.

2 pounds ground beef
1 green pepper, chopped
6 tomatoes or 2 14½-ounce cans stewed tomatoes
6 ounces tomato paste
2 onions, chopped
1⅓ cups water
½ teaspoon oregano
3 cloves garlic
2 jalapeño peppers, chopped
1 cup dark raisins
salt and pepper to taste
tortilla chips

Optional ingredients:
6 ounces tomato sauce
frozen hash browns or diced potatoes
1 cup slivered almonds

Brown ground beef, crumble, and drain off fat. Add all ingredients (including optional tomato sauce) except tortilla chips, almonds, and potatoes. Cover and simmer 30 minutes or more using moderate heat. Serve hot in chafing dish. It can be frozen and reheated in microwave or oven.

If potatoes are used, add at end of simmering process and cook until potatoes are done. Do not freeze with potatoes in it. Sprinkle almonds on top when serving, if desired. Serve with tortilla chips for dipping.

Makes 8 servings.

TEX-MEX DIP

Senator **Nancy Landon Kassebaum**—*Kansas*

This is a colorful layer dip which was adapted from a recipe in a magazine. Tex-Mex dip is now included in all Kassebaum office parties. In fact, one staff member has suggested that we have a bring-your-own-dip party.

8 ounces sour cream
1 package powdered taco mix
2 cans jalapeño-flavored bean dip
2 packages frozen guacamole dip

Toppings:
2 tomatoes, seeded and chopped
½ cup black olives, chopped
¼ cup green onions, chopped
1 cup cheddar cheese, grated

Mix sour cream and taco mix. Spread the bean dip on a large platter. Spread guacamole dip almost to the edge of the bean dip. Spread the sour cream mixture on top of the guacamole layer. Generously sprinkle the toppings over the sour cream. Serve with corn or tortilla chips.

Makes 24 servings.

VICTORY PARTY
LAYERED DIP

Representative **Wes Watkins**—*Oklahoma*

This is great served with large-sized Fritos!

2 **tomatoes**
3 **16-ounce cans bean dip**
2 **large avocados**
1 **teaspoon lemon juice**
   salt to taste
2 **cups sour cream**
1 **package taco seasoning**
4 **green onions, chopped**
1 **can black olives**
10 **ounces cheddar cheese, grated**

Chop tomatoes and drain on paper towel. Set aside.

Spread bean dip on a plate or tray at least 12 inches in diameter. Mash the avocados and season with lemon juice and salt. Spread on bean-dip layer. Mix sour cream in taco seasoning and spread on avocado layer. Add tomato chunks, green onions, olives, and cheddar cheese.

Makes 24 servings.

CHEESE STRAWS

Senator **Howell Heflin**—*Alabama*

This particular appetizer freezes well and can be ready in minutes for unexpected guests.

1 **pound sharp cheddar cheese, grated**
½ **cup margarine**
2 **cups sifted flour**
½ **teaspoon salt**
¼ **teaspoon red pepper**
¼ **teaspoon paprika**

Soften cheese and margarine at room temperature. Mix well. Add dry ingredients and mix well. Place mixture in cheese straw press and press onto ungreased cookie sheets. Cut into 4-inch pieces before cooking. Bake at 350° for about 15 minutes, or until dried out but not brown.

Makes about 90 4-inch straws.

APPETIZER PIE

Senator **Connie Mack**—*Florida*

This is a great dip and will disappear at any party!

8 ounces cream cheese
2 tablespoons milk
2½ ounces dried chipped beef
2 tablespoons instant minced onion
2 tablespoons green pepper, chopped
pepper to taste
½ cup sour cream
⅛ cup chopped nuts

Combine ingredients in a casserole dish. Bake at 350° for 15 minutes. Remove and serve with favorite crackers.

Makes 12 servings.

MUSTARD SAUCE

Senator **Charles Grassley**—*Iowa*

*We've enjoyed this treat with
Sue, a former Des Moines girl.
Her backyard adjoins ours.*

Make a paste of the following ingredients:
  4 tablespoons dry mustard
  1 tablespoon butter
  ¼ cup water
Add:
  6 tablespoons sugar
  6 tablespoons white vinegar
Bring to a boil and add:
  1 beaten egg

Cook until thick. Refrigerate. Pour over an 8-ounce block of cream cheese. Serve with crackers.

Makes 20 servings.

CHEESE BALL

Senator Charles Grassley—*Iowa*

Best if made a little ahead, so flavors can blend. Serve with crackers.

16 ounces cream cheese, softened
1 package Good Seasons Italian salad-dressing mix, dry
1 cup chopped pecans

Mix cream cheese, salad-dressing mix, and ½ cup chopped nuts. Shape into two balls and roll in the remaining chopped pecans.

Makes 24 servings.

FIESTA CHEESE WHEEL

Senator **Christopher Bond**—*Missouri*

Great for a tailgate party before a Cardinals or Chiefs football game.

14½ ounces canned whole plum tomatoes, drained
 8 ounces cream cheese, softened
 8 ounces cheddar cheese, grated
 ½ cup butter, softened
 ½ cup onion, finely chopped
 2 cloves garlic, crushed
 1 teaspoon salt
 ¼ teaspoon cayenne pepper
 ⅛ teaspoon cumin
 ¾ cup walnuts, chopped
    fresh parsley, chopped

Seed tomatoes and dry between paper towels. Combine tomatoes, cheeses, butter, onion, garlic, salt, cayenne pepper, and cumin. Beat until smooth. Spoon mixture onto a large piece of waxed paper. Shape into a wheel approximately 1 inch thick. Chill until firm. Cover wheel with chopped walnuts. Sprinkle with parsley. Serve as an appetizer with crackers or tortilla chips.

Makes 20 servings.

STUFFED MUSHROOMS

Representative **Dante Fascell**—*Florida*

I enjoy it as a hot hors d'oeuvre or as a vegetable to accompany a meal.

1 pint large, fresh mushrooms
¾ cup bread crumbs
¼ cup grated Parmesan or Romano cheese
chopped parsley
olive oil

Wipe off the mushrooms with a damp cloth and remove stems. Place caps underside up in a baking dish. Cut the stems up finely and mix with bread crumbs, cheese, and parsley. Fill each mushroom cup with the crumb and cheese mixture and drizzle 1 or 2 drops of oil onto the top of each. Add ⅛ to ¼ inch of water to bottom of baking dish and cover with foil. Bake at 350° for 25–30 minutes. You may prepare as above and freeze before cooking.

Makes 20 servings.

CRAB-STUFFED MUSHROOMS

Delegate **Ben Blaz**—*Guam*

12 ounces crabmeat
½ pound mushrooms, with medium to large
   caps
3 spring onions
1 tablespoon margarine
2 teaspoons lemon juice
1 teaspoon dry mustard
   dash ground red pepper
¼ cup mayonnaise
2 tablespoons yogurt

Remove any shell fragments from crabmeat. Rinse
mushrooms and remove stems from caps. Chop
stems and onions, including some of the green.
Sauté in margarine until soft. Stir in crabmeat and
remaining ingredients. Stuff mushroom caps. Broil
until lightly browned.

Makes 10 servings.

SWEET AND SOUR MEATBALLS

Senator **Christopher Bond**—*Missouri*

We were still newlyweds when Kit ran for the U.S. Congress in 1968, and our first parade of that campaign was during the Hermann Maifest. Following the event, we were invited to a reception where these savory meatballs were served. Featuring pork and soy, two of Missouri's major agricultural products, they are always a popular item on a buffet table.

5 **pounds ground chuck**
1 **pound ground pork**
4 **eggs**
4 **teaspoons salt**
2 **teaspoons pepper**
1 **teaspoon nutmeg**
3 **tablespoons seasoning salt**
4 **cups light cream**
1 **large onion, finely chopped**
12 **ounces bread crumbs**
Sweet and sour sauce:
4 **13-ounce cans chunked pineapple**
½ **cup cornstarch**
1 **cup red wine vinegar**
2 **cups brown sugar**
¼ **cup soy sauce**
1 **green pepper, finely diced**

Combine all meatball ingredients. Shape mixture into balls about 1 inch in diameter. Brown in vegetable oil. Drain, cool, and refrigerate.

For sauce, drain pineapple, retaining juice. Add enough water to juice to make 4 cups. Dissolve cornstarch in vinegar. Combine all ingredients, except green pepper. Cook, stirring constantly, until thickened. Add green pepper. Heat thoroughly. To serve, heat meatballs in sauce. Transfer to a chafing dish.

Makes 9 dozen.

CHARLESTON EGG BALLS

Senator **Ernest F. Hollings**—*South Carolina*

Since butter is used instead of mayonnaise, there is less chance of spoiling. This was important in the warm climate of Charleston prior to refrigeration and air conditioning.

8 **hard-boiled eggs, cooled**
½ **cup butter**
1 **teaspoon salt**
¼ **teaspoon red pepper**
½ **teaspoon Worcestershire sauce**
¼ **teaspoon celery seed**
1 **cup bread crumbs**

Using an electric mixer or food processor, cream eggs and butter until well blended. Add salt, pepper, Worcestershire sauce, and celery seed. Refrigerate several hours. Form mixture into 1-inch balls, then roll in bread crumbs.

Makes 30 balls.

Salads

FRUIT SALAD

Vice President **J. Danforth Quayle**

> **apple pieces**
> **melon balls**
> **orange sections**
> **grapefruit sections**
> **strawberries**
> **pear pieces**
> **bananas, sliced**
> **grapes, red and green seedless**
> **coconut, shredded**
> **1 cup nuts, chopped**
> **kiwifruit, sliced for garnish**

Mix together 6 cups of your favorite combination of fresh fruits with coconut and nuts.

Orange vanilla dressing:
> **1 cup vanilla yogurt**
> **2 tablespoons frozen orange juice concentrate**

Stir yogurt and concentrate until well blended. Combine with fruit mixture. Chill until served.

Serve on lettuce leaves and garnish with kiwifruit slices.

Makes 12 servings.

ORANGE AND ONION SALAD

Representative **Vic Fazio**—*California*

This is a nice accompaniment to Italian or Mediterranean dishes.

6 **large, firm, juicy oranges**
3 **tablespoons red wine vinegar**
6 **tablespoons high-quality olive oil**
1 **teaspoon dried oregano**
1 **medium purple onion, peeled and sliced paper-thin**
1 **cup imported black olives (Niçoise, Kalamata, or Alfonso)**
¼ **cup fresh chives, snipped**
  black pepper to taste

Peel the oranges and cut each into 4 or 5 crosswise slices. Transfer oranges to a shallow serving dish and sprinkle them with the vinegar, olive oil, and oregano. Toss gently, cover and refrigerate for 30 minutes. Toss the oranges again, arrange the sliced oranges, black olives, and onion attractively on serving dish or individual salad plates. Sprinkle with chives and ground pepper.

Makes 8 servings.

RASPBERRY-BLUEBERRY SALAD

Representative **William Goodling**—*Pennsylvania*

 2 3-ounce boxes raspberry gelatin
 1 envelope plain gelatin
 ½ cup cold water
 1 cup half-and-half
 1 cup sugar
 ½ teaspoon vanilla
 8 ounces cream cheese
 ½ cup black walnuts
 1 cup hot water
 1 20-ounce can blueberry pie filling

Layer 1: Dissolve 1 small box of raspberry gelatin in a 9 x 13 dish according to directions and let set.

Layer 2: Dissolve envelope of plain gelatin in cold water. Heat half-and-half and sugar, then mix in gelatin. Add vanilla and cream cheese and beat well. While warm, add black walnuts. Pour this mixture over the first layer and let set.

Layer 3: Dissolve the remaining raspberry gelatin in 1 cup of hot water. Add blueberry pie filling, cool, and pour over second layer.

Makes 24 servings.

MUSHROOM AND SPINACH SALAD

Senator **James A. McClure**—*Idaho*

> 1 10-ounce package fresh spinach
> 6 strips lean bacon, crisply fried
> 1 bunch scallions or onions, sliced
> ¼ pound fresh mushrooms, cleaned and sliced

Dressing:

> 1 egg yolk
> 2 teaspoons lemon juice
> ½ teaspoon salt
> 1 clove garlic, minced
> ¼ teaspoon sugar
> ⅛ teaspoon dry mustard
> ⅛ teaspoon black pepper
> 6 tablespoons salad oil

Clean and thoroughly dry spinach and place in a salad bowl. Crumble bacon over spinach. Add onions and mushrooms. Cover with plastic wrap and chill. Toss lightly before serving. Combine ingredients for dressing and blend. Pour as desired over mushroom and spinach salad.

Makes 6 servings.

GARDEN VEGETABLE SALAD

Representative **Beverly Byron**—*Maryland*

    6 Shredded Wheat biscuits, crushed
    2 tomatoes, chopped
    1 cucumber, chopped
    2 green peppers, chopped
    2 bunches scallions, sliced
    ½ cup parsley
Dressing:
    2 cloves garlic, chopped
    1 tablespoon dill
    ½ cup lemon juice
    ½ cup olive oil
      salt and pepper to taste

Combine salad ingredients in a large bowl and mix together. Mix dressing ingredients together and toss over salad. Refrigerate 6 hours or more and serve.

Makes 6 servings.

COLD SOMEN SALAD

Senator **Spark Matsunaga**—*Hawaii*

   1 **9-ounce package somen (noodles)**
   1 **cup chicken broth**
   ¼ **cup sugar**
   ¼ **cup soy sauce**
   ¼ **cup rice vinegar**
   2 **tablespoons sesame oil**
   ¼ **pound crab (or imitation crab) or cooked**
         shrimp
   ¼ **pound ham, julienned**
   1 **small cucumber, slivered**
   2 **cups shredded lettuce**
   4 **scallions, chopped**
         fresh coriander sprigs

Cook somen according to directions on the package. Rinse and drain. Chill. Combine broth, sugar, soy sauce, vinegar, and oil. Bring to a boil. Reduce heat and simmer 5 minutes. Chill. To serve, place somen on large platter. Garnish with remaining ingredients. Serve with broth mixture.

Makes 6 to 8 servings.

APPLE AND SHRIMP SALAD

Senator **Steve Symms**—*Idaho*

> **14** ounces jumbo shrimp, deveined
> **2** medium Idaho onions
> **2** Red or Golden Delicious apples
> lettuce
> watercress

Caper mayonnaise:

> **¾** cup mayonnaise
> **2** tablespoons capers

Drain and rinse shrimp. Slice onions and separate into rings. Core apples and slice in rings. Arrange salad greens on 4 serving plates. Place apple slices in center of each plate. Arrange shrimp and onion rings around apple slices. Mix ingredients for caper mayonnaise and serve over apple and shrimp salad.

Makes 4 servings.

HEALTHY COLD TURKEY SALAD

Representative **Barbara Boxer**—*California*

2 cups white turkey meat, cubed
¼ cup sweet red onion, chopped
½ cup red or yellow bell pepper, chopped
½ cup water chestnuts or jicama, chopped
¼ cup walnuts, chopped
　freshly ground black pepper to taste

Dressing:

¼ cup yogurt
¼ cup light mayonnaise
1 teaspoon dill weed
¼ cup parsley, minced
　salt to taste
1 tablespoon lemon juice

Mix salad ingredients and toss lightly. Combine dressing items and pour over salad. Chill.

Makes 6 servings.

CURRIED CHICKEN SALAD

Senator **Christopher Bond**—*Missouri*

Following our son Sam's christening at the First Presbyterian Church in my hometown of Mexico, this savory chicken salad was featured along with asparagus and a watermelon basket brimming with fresh fruit.

That Father's Day in 1981 is a date we'll never forget.

2 cups cooked chicken breast, diced
4 scallions, sliced
1 cup water chestnuts, sliced
2 cups cooked rice, at room temperature
1 cup mayonnaise
½ cup prepared chutney
1 teaspoon curry powder
1 teaspoon salt
 freshly ground pepper to taste
2 bananas
¼ cup lemon juice
1½ cups chopped peanuts

Combine chicken, scallions, and water chestnuts with rice. In a separate bowl, combine mayonnaise, chutney, curry, salt, and pepper. Mix well. Thoroughly combine mayonnaise dressing with chicken-rice mixture. Chill. Taste and adjust seasonings. Cut bananas diagonally into 1-inch slices. Dip slices into lemon juice and coat with peanuts.

To serve, arrange salad on small platter. Surround salad with banana slices and garnish with chopped nuts. Additional condiments may be served: chopped green peppers, toasted almonds, plumped raisins, and coconut are a few choices.

Makes 6 to 8 servings.

CAESAR SALAD

Representative **Tony Hall**—*Ohio*

1 clove garlic, peeled
salt
1 teaspoon dry mustard
1 teaspoon lemon juice
3 tablespoons olive oil
3 bunches romaine lettuce
1 tablespoon grated Parmesan cheese
1 can anchovies, drained
1 egg, boiled for 1 minute
½ cup croutons

Rub garlic on bottom of a wooden salad bowl and sprinkle with salt. Add the mustard, lemon juice, and olive oil and stir rapidly until the liquid blends evenly.

Wash the lettuce well and dry the leaves. Tear leaves into small pieces and add them to the bowl. Sprinkle with Parmesan cheese. Add anchovies and break the egg over the salad. Sprinkle with the croutons and mix thoroughly with a wooden spoon.

Makes 10 servings.

SPINACH SALAD

Representative **James Sensenbrenner**—*Wisconsin*

Dressing:
- 1 cup oil
- ⅓ cup vinegar
- ½ cup sugar
- 1 tablespoon celery seed
- 1 teaspoon salt
- 1 tablespoon dry mustard
- 2 green onions, sliced

Spinach salad:
- 2 heads Boston lettuce
- 2 avocados, peeled and cut in wedges
- 1 Bermuda onion, thinly sliced
- 1 pound fresh spinach
- 11 ounces mandarin oranges, drained

Combine all dressing ingredients, except onions, in blender and blend thoroughly. Stir in onions. Chill several hours. Tear greens into bite-size pieces and add remaining salad ingredients. Add enough dressing to moisten and toss lightly.

Makes 12 servings.

SUMMER RICE SALAD

Senator **Christopher Bond**—*Missouri*

The diversity of Missouri agriculture is possibly most apparent in the Boot heel. In this southeast corner of the state you will discover cotton and rice as well as the more typical corn and soybean crops. A barbecue in conjunction with the Sikeston Cotton Carnival yielded this summer sensation.

3 cups cooked rice, cooled
¼ cup mayonnaise
½ cup radishes, thinly sliced
½ cup scallions, thinly sliced
1 sweet red pepper, minced
1 green pepper, minced
2 tablespoons sweet gherkins, minced
1 tablespoon fresh parsley, minced
1 tablespoon fresh dill, chopped
1 tablespoon fresh chives, snipped

Dressing:
½ cup fresh lemon juice
2 teaspoons salt
2 garlic cloves, crushed
1¼ cups salad oil

Combine first 10 ingredients and mix well, then set aside. Place lemon juice, salt, and garlic in a food processor or blender, mix well. With machine running, add oil in a thin stream until thoroughly incorporated. (If added too fast, dressing may separate.) Add dressing to rice mixture and season with salt and pepper. Taste and adjust seasoning. Refrigerate and allow to return to room temperature before serving. Mound on lettuce leaves and garnish with black olives or red pepper rings.

Makes 8 to 10 servings.

PASTA SALAD

Senator **Richard Lugar**—*Indiana*

This is an ideal dish for a potluck supper.

1 **pound spaghetti**
1 **green pepper**
1 **bunch green onions**
2 **stalks celery**
2 **tomatoes**
1 **cucumber**
8 **ounces bottled Italian dressing**
1 **jar McCormick's Salad Supreme**

Break spaghetti into bite-sized pieces and cook. Chop vegetables finely. Drain pasta and add all other ingredients. Mix together while pasta is still warm. Best when made a day ahead and refrigerated. Serve cold or at room temperature.

Makes 15 to 20 servings.

Soups and Stews

Chowders

Bisques

Stews

Chili

ALL-AMERICAN CLAM CHOWDER

President **George Bush**

> 3 slices bacon
> ½ cup minced onions
> 1 7½-ounce can minced clams (save clam liquor)
> 1 cup cubed potatoes
> 1 10¾-ounce can cream of celery soup
> 1½ cups milk
> dash of pepper

Fry bacon until crisp. Remove and break into 1-inch pieces. Brown onion in bacon fat. Add clam liquor and potatoes. Cover and cook over low heat until potatoes are done (about 15 minutes). Blend in bacon pieces, minced clams, and other ingredients. Heat, but do not boil. Bacon may be used for garnish.

Makes 6 servings.

NEW ENGLAND
CLAM CHOWDER

Representative **Paul Kanjorski**—*Pennsylvania*

¼ pound salt bacon
1 large Spanish onion, chopped
3 bottles Doxsee clam juice (6–8 ounces each)
4 large potatoes, peeled and sliced
21 ounces whole baby clams
1½ quarts half-and-half
oyster crackers

Finely chop bacon and begin browning. Add onion and brown until clear. Add clam juice, potatoes, and clams to mixture and heat until potatoes are tender. Add half-and-half and heat until close to boiling. If necessary, add regular milk to dilute to desired consistency. Serve immediately with oyster crackers.

Note: Do not add half-and-half until ready to serve. Before adding milk, the mixture may even be refrigerated until serving time.

Makes 12 servings.

CAPE COD FISH CHOWDER

Senator **Edward Kennedy**—*Massachusetts*

Even if you have never walked the beach at Cape Cod, the thought conjures up fleets of fishing boats and favorite foods of the Cape. Enjoy this hearty New England favorite of mine!

2 **pounds fresh haddock**
2 **ounces salt pork, diced (or 2 tablespoons butter or margarine)**
2 **medium onions, sliced**
1 **cup celery, chopped**
4 **large potatoes, diced**
1 **bay leaf, crumbled**
1 **quart milk**
2 **tablespoons butter or margarine**
1 **teaspoon salt**
freshly ground black pepper to taste

Simmer haddock in 2 cups of water for 15 minutes. Drain off and reserve broth. Remove skin and bones from fish.

Sauté diced salt pork in a large pot until crisp. Remove cooked salt pork. Sauté onions in pork fat or butter until golden brown. Add fish, celery, potatoes, and bay leaf.

Measure reserved fish broth plus enough boiling water to make 3 cups liquid. Add to pot and simmer for 30 minutes. Add milk and butter and simmer for an additional 5 minutes, or until well heated. Add salt and pepper to taste.

Makes 8 servings.

BACON AND BEAN CHOWDER

Senator **Charles Grassley**—*Iowa*

Florence is one of the best cooks I know, and I'm sure that she won't mind sharing her recipe with you.

1 cup navy or pea beans, dried
1 quart water
6 slices diced bacon
1 onion, chopped
2 teaspoons pepper
1⅓ cups potato, diced
1⅓ cups diced celery, including leaves
1½ cups carrots, sliced
1 29-ounce can tomatoes
2 tablespoons flour
2 cups hot milk
   dried parsley
   grated American cheese

Combine beans and water in a large kettle. Bring to a boil and cook for 2 minutes. Remove from heat and let stand for 1 hour. Cook bacon and onion until lightly browned. Add, with fat, to beans. Bring to a boil again. Cover and simmer for 1 hour. Add potato, celery, carrots, and tomatoes. Simmer 30 minutes longer. Blend flour with a little cold water and stir into soup. Cook until slightly thickened. Add hot milk and additional seasoning, if necessary. Stir in dried parsley and cheese.

Makes about 2 quarts.

ROSEMONT FARM CHOWDER

Senator **John Heinz**—*Pennsylvania*

We enjoy it with a little Tabasco and onion salt. It is very good served hot or cold.

1 **20-ounce bag of frozen "le sueur" peas**
1 **20-ounce bag of frozen baby corn, white**
1½ **cups chicken broth**
1 **tablespoon butter**

Defrost peas and corn. Bring vegetables, broth, and butter almost to a boil in a saucepan. Blend mixture well in blender and strain. Heat on stove for 5 minutes. Make sure that the color does not change. Cream may be added if desired.

Makes 8 servings.

CRAB BISQUE

Senator **Robert Dole**—*Kansas*

- **1 10½-ounce can cream of mushroom soup**
- **1 10½-ounce can cream of asparagus soup**
- **5 ounces milk**
- **1 cup light cream**
- **1 7½-ounce can crabmeat, flaked and cartilage removed**
- **¼ cup dry white wine**

Blend soups and stir in milk and cream. Heat just to boiling and add crabmeat. Heat thoroughly. Stir in wine just before serving. May be frozen.

Makes 6 to 8 servings.

SEAFOOD GUMBO

Senator **John Breaux**—*Louisiana*

>   1 cup flour
>   1 cup cooking oil
>   2½ quarts hot water
>   2 cups onion, chopped
>   ½ cup green onion tops, chopped
>   ¼ cup parsley, chopped
>   1 tablespoon salt
>   1 teaspoon cayenne or red pepper
>   1 pound crabmeat, or 2 cans crabmeat
>   2 pounds shrimp, raw and peeled
>   1 pint oysters with liquid

To make roux, mix flour and oil together in a 4-cup measure. Microwave on high for 7 minutes. Stir well. Microwave on high for 30 seconds. Stir again and cook 30 seconds more. Roux will be a dark caramel color.

To make gumbo, add hot water, roux, onion, green onion tops, parsley, salt, and pepper to a large cooking pot. Cover and cook on high for 15 minutes. Add crabmeat, shrimp, and oysters and cook on medium for 20 minutes. Serve as a soup with rice.

LENTIL SOUP

Senator **Alfonse D'Amato**—*New York*

Fighting inflation at the supermarket may be the toughest battle of all for "the forgotten middle class." Most of the federal regulations that stifle business and private enterprise are passed right along to us—the consumer—in the form of higher prices at the check-out counter.

Over the years, I have discovered that many of my family's favorite dishes are not only easy to prepare, but also economical. More importantly, they are flavorful and nutritious.

Enjoy these "recipes for the forgotten middle class." By sharing our favorites with you, I hope they will help ease the pinch on your family's food budget.

1 **cup lentils**
4 **slices bacon, cut in small pieces**
1 **clove garlic**
3 **tablespoons tomato sauce**
2 **cups water**
1 **tablespoon fresh parsley, chopped**
  salt and pepper

Wash lentils under cold water. Drain. Sauté bacon in large saucepan with garlic clove until garlic is golden brown. Remove garlic. Stir in tomato sauce. Add water. Let soup base cook until rolling boil. Add lentils to base. Let cook over medium heat, adding more water as needed during cooking. Cook for 30–45 minutes until lentils are tender. Add fresh parsley. Add salt and ground pepper to taste.

Note: Small, boiled pasta may be added to soup before serving.

Makes 3 servings.

INSTANT MEATBALL SOUP

Senator **Alfonse D'Amato**—*New York*

4 cups water
2 large carrots, peeled and cubed
3 large celery stalks, diced
1 medium onion, diced
4 chicken bouillon cubes
½ pound ground beef
   salt and pepper
½ cup grated cheese, Romano or Parmesan

Boil water in large saucepan or soup kettle. Add carrots, celery, and onion. Cover and let cook until vegetables are tender. Add bouillon cubes and simmer.

Season ground beef with salt and pepper. Shape beef into tiny meatballs of ½-inch diameter. Add meatballs to soup and cook from 3 to 5 minutes. Serve with grated cheese.

Note: Boiled pasta or rice may be added before serving.

Makes 3 servings.

CURRIED PEA SOUP

Senator **Christopher Bond**—*Missouri*

Equally good hot or cold, this flavorful soup is often served from a thermos on float trips on the Niangua and for tailgates at Faurot Field in Columbia.

1 **10-ounce package frozen peas**
1 **medium onion, sliced**
1 **small carrot, sliced**
1 **rib of celery with leaves, sliced**
1 **medium potato, sliced**
1 **garlic clove, crushed**
1 **teaspoon salt**
1 **teaspoon curry powder**
2 **cups chicken stock, divided**
1 **cup heavy cream**

Place vegetables, seasonings, and 1 cup of stock in a saucepan and bring to a boil. Cover, reduce heat, and simmer 20 to 30 minutes until vegetables are very tender. Transfer vegetables to a food processor or blender. Puree. With the motor running, pour in remaining stock and the cream. Chill. Garnish each portion with whipped cream and a mint leaf.

To serve hot, omit adding cream in food processor or blender. Instead, process puree and stock only. Heat. Remove from heat and stir in cream. Garnish with a teaspoon of sour cream and crisply cooked, crumbled bacon.

Makes 4 to 6 servings.

CAULIFLOWER SOUP

Senator **Joseph Lieberman**—*Connecticut*

Soup is a favorite beginning to a Czechoslovakian meal. It is usually served with tasty additions like the cauliflower.

3 **tablespoons butter or margarine**
3 **tablespoons all-purpose flour**
⅛ **teaspoon nutmeg**
3⅔ **cups chicken broth**
1 **cup water**
3 **cups small cauliflowerets**
1 **egg yolk**
3 **tablespoons heavy cream**
   snipped fresh parsley

In a medium saucepan, melt butter or margarine and blend in flour and nutmeg. Slowly stir in broth and water, then bring to a boil while stirring. Add cauliflowerets. Simmer soup, covered, about 25 minutes, or until cauliflowerets are tender.

In a small bowl, mix egg yolk with cream, stirring until blended. Add to soup. Bring soup just to boiling point, stirring constantly. Serve in small bowls. Sprinkle with parsley.

Makes 6 servings.

WATERCRESS SOUP

Senator **Christopher Bond**—*Missouri*

While I fish for trout from the back of the canoe, my wife usually is at the bow searching for watercress. A fall float trip on the Eleven Point River yielded a bumper crop and led to the development of this refreshing soup. We enjoy it as a prelude to a light luncheon or patio supper.

6 cups watercress
3 tablespoons butter, divided
¼ cup minced onion
1½ cups water
1 teaspoon salt
½ teaspoon white pepper
½ teaspoon curry powder
2 tablespoons flour
2 14½-ounce cans chicken broth
2 cups milk
2 egg yolks
1 cup heavy cream

Rinse and drain watercress. Remove coarsest stems. Reserve. Melt 1 tablespoon butter in a large saucepan. Add onion and cook until golden. Add watercress, water, salt, pepper, and curry. Cook over high heat 5 minutes. Transfer mixture to a food processor or blender. Puree. Melt remaining 2 tablespoons butter in a saucepan and stir in flour. Add chicken broth and milk, bring to a boil. Stir in watercress mixture. Combine egg yolks and heavy cream and beat until slightly thickened. Stir 1 cup of hot soup into egg/cream mixture. Add to remaining soup, stirring constantly. Heat, but do not boil. Garnish with croutons and a sprig of watercress.

Makes 8 servings.

SENATE BEAN SOUP

Senator **Carl Levin**—*Michigan*

Whatever uncertainties may exist in the Senate of the United States, one thing is sure: Bean Soup is on the menu of the Senate Restaurant every day.

The origin of this culinary decree has been lost in antiquity, but there are several oft-repeated legends.

One story has it that Senator Fred Thomas Dubois of Idaho, who served in the Senate from 1901 to 1907, when chairman of the committee that supervised the Senate Restaurant, gaveled through a resolution requiring that bean soup be on the menu every day.

Another account attributes the bean soup mandate to Senator Knute Nelson of Minnesota, who expressed his fondness for it in 1903.

In any case, senators and their guests are always assured of a hearty, nourishing dish; they know they can rely upon its delightful flavor and epicurean qualities.

2 pounds small Michigan Navy beans
4 quarts hot water
1½ pounds smoked ham hocks
1 tablespoon butter
1 onion, chopped
    salt and pepper to taste

Wash and sort beans and run through hot water until beans are white again. Put beans on the fire with hot water. Add ham hocks and boil slowly for 3 hours in a covered pot. Braise the onion in a little butter. When light brown, add to the bean soup. Season with salt and pepper when ready to serve.

Makes 8 servings.

HAMBURGER SOUP

Representative **Rod Chandler**—*Washington*

- **1 pound ground beef**
- **1 cup onion, chopped**
- **3 cups water**
- **1 cup carrots, chopped**
- **1 cup celery, diced**
- **1 cup mushrooms, sliced**
- **1 cup potatoes, cubed**
- **1 teaspoon Kitchen Bouquet**
- **1 bay leaf**
- **1 28-ounce can tomatoes**

In a large saucepan, cook and stir meat until brown. Drain off fat. Cook and stir onion with meat until onion is tender, about 5 minutes. Stir in remaining ingredients and heat to boiling. Reduce heat and cover. Simmer for 30 minutes. May be frozen.

Makes 6 servings.

SAUSAGE-ZUCCHINI SOUP

Senator **Christopher Bond**—*Missouri*

During a visit to Rolla for the annual St. Patrick's Day festivities, we sampled this substantial and satisfying soup at the home of a friend. Ladle into sizable soup bowls and serve in front of a crackling fire.

1¼ pounds mild Italian sausage without casings
1½ cups celery, sliced
4 pounds fresh tomatoes, peeled and cut in wedges
1½ cups tomato juice
1 teaspoon salt
1½ teaspoons Italian seasonings (or a mixture of basil and oregano)
1 teaspoon sugar
¼ teaspoon garlic salt
2 green peppers, cut into 1-inch pieces
1½ pounds zucchini, cut into ¼-inch slices
1 cup shredded mozzarella cheese

Crumble sausage into a 4-quart saucepan, brown, drain off fat. Add celery, cook 10 minutes. Add tomatoes, juice, and seasonings and simmer for 10 minutes. Stir in green peppers, cook for 5 minutes. Add zucchini and cook 1 to 2 minutes, until barely heated. Caution: Do not overcook zucchini. Sprinkle mozzarella cheese over the top. Serve immediately.

Note: If more liquid is desired, add more tomato juice. Two 28-ounce cans Italian plum tomatoes may be substituted for fresh tomatoes.

Makes 8 to 10 servings.

KENTUCKY VEGETABLE BEEF SOUP

Senator **Wendell Ford**—*Kentucky*

1 pound beef soup meat
5 quarts water
1 bunch celery, diced
2 large onions, sliced
2 large carrots, diced
2 large potatoes, diced
1 16-ounce package frozen mixed
   vegetables
1 16-ounce can tomatoes, mashed
4 teaspoons salt
1 teaspoon pepper
1 cup uncooked macaroni

Simmer soup meat in water for 2 hours in large covered pan. Add celery, onions, carrots, potatoes, frozen vegetables, tomatoes, and seasonings. Let this simmer for at least 1 hour. Add macaroni and cook 30 minutes more. Test to see if seasonings suit taste. Freezes very well.

Makes 6 quarts and yields 12 servings.

MISSOURI APPLE SOUP

Senator **Christopher Bond**—*Missouri*

Stephenson's Apple Orchard in eastern Jackson County is a name that brings to mind family outings during the fall picking season and bushel baskets heaping with succulent apples.

2 tablespoons butter
2 medium onions, thinly sliced
6 red Jonathan apples—peeled, cored, and diced
4 cups chicken broth
2 tablespoons sugar
1 tablespoon curry powder
  salt and freshly ground white pepper to taste
1 to 2 cups light cream

In a Dutch oven, melt butter and sauté onions until transparent. Add apples, broth, sugar, and curry powder. Season with salt and pepper. Cook covered over low heat until apples are soft. Strain apples and onions from broth and reserve. Set broth aside. Place apples and onions in a food processor or blender; puree. Add broth, blend well. Add cream according to desired richness. Chill. Taste and adjust seasoning. Garnish with thin apple wedges and a sprinkling of sliced almonds.

Makes 10 to 12 servings.

POLISH SAUSAGE STEW

Senator **Chuck Grassley**—*Iowa*

Jolene, our friend, brought this to our house for supper one night.

1 can cream of celery soup
⅓ cup light brown sugar
1 large can sauerkraut, drained
2 pounds Polish sausage, cut in chunks
4 medium potatoes, cubed
1 cup onion, chopped
1 cup Monterey Jack cheese, shredded

Combine in a crockpot the soup, sugar, and sauerkraut. Add the sausage, potatoes, and onion. Cook on low for 8 hours, or on high for 4 hours. Skim off fat and stir in cheese just before serving.

Makes 4 to 6 servings.

NEBRASKA BEEF STEW

Representative **Virginia Smith**—*Nebraska*

This recipe features my favorite Nebraska beef and pork.

1½ **pounds boneless beef, cut into 12 chunks**
6 **slices bacon, cut in half**
  flour to dredge the meat
2 **tablespoons bacon grease**
12 **small onions, peeled**
1 **tablespoon flour**
1½ **cups beef consommé**
½ **cup cooking wine**
1 **cup carrots, sliced**

Roll each piece of beef in the ½ slice of bacon. Fasten with toothpicks. Dredge lightly in flour. Melt the bacon grease and brown the beef and onions. Remove meat and onions from the pan and remove toothpicks. Pour off all but 1 tablespoon of fat. Stir in 1 tablespoon of flour. Add the consommé and wine and stir until smooth. Add beef, onions, and carrots. Simmer for 1½ to 2 hours until the meat is very tender. Season to taste. Serve on buttered wide noodles.

Makes 3 servings.

BUSY-DAY STEW

Senator **Spark Matsunaga**—*Hawaii*

2 pounds stew meat, cubed
2 potatoes, cubed
1 bunch carrots, chopped
1 cup celery, chopped
2 large onions, chopped
¼ cup green pepper, chopped
1 teaspoon salt
   pepper to taste
1 tablespoon sugar
3 tablespoons quick tapioca
2 tablespoons red wine

Place ingredients in large covered crockpot in order given. No need to brown meat. Stir twice. Cook for 5 hours at 250°. Uncover the last 30 minutes if the stew seems too moist.

Makes 6 to 8 servings.

BEEF STEW

Representative **Beryl Anthony**—*Arkansas*

3 to 4	pounds lean stew meat (chuck roast is great)
2	tablespoons olive oil
2 to 3	ribs of celery, cut in 1-inch lengths
5	carrots, cut in 1-inch lengths
2 or 3	onions, diced
5	potatoes, diced
	salt and pepper to taste
2	tablespoons sugar
3	tablespoons minute tapioca
2	bay leaves
3	cups tomato juice
1	clove garlic, minced
½	cup red wine
2	cups frozen green peas
1	cup fresh mushrooms, sliced

Preheat oven to 250°. Sauté meat lightly in olive oil. Place all ingredients in pot except frozen peas and mushrooms. Seal pot with foil and put lid on. Bake for 4½ hours at 250°. Add peas and mushrooms and cook 30 minutes longer.

Makes 6 servings.

CHILI

Senator **John Glenn**—*Ohio*

4 onions
2 tablespoons olive oil
9 pounds ground beef
1 15-ounce can chili
4 22-ounce cans chili beans
⅓ cup chili powder
3 14½-ounce cans stewed tomatoes
1 large tomato, cut in small pieces

Chop onions in small pieces and brown in hot olive oil. Brown the ground beef after the onions have cooked in the frying pan. Put the chili, chili beans, and chili powder in a stewing pot. Add the browned ground beef and onions. Add tomatoes. Simmer for 2 hours.

Makes 24 servings.

Annie Glenn likes to make the chili the day before as it helps to meld the flavors. It can be made in a turkey roaster and is great topped with grated cheese, sour cream, and fresh chopped onions and tomatoes.

FRESH BERRY SOUP

Representative **Beverly Byron**—*Maryland*

This is a healthful soup or a lovely dessert.

2 cups orange juice
2 cups vanilla yogurt
1 tablespoon honey
2 tablespoons lemon juice
1¾ pints fresh blueberries or strawberries
¼ teaspoon cinnamon
⅛ teaspoon nutmeg

Mix all ingredients together in a blender. Chill. Place a few berries in bowls. Ladle soup on top. Garnish with fresh mint.

Makes 8 to 10 servings.

Side Dishes

Vegetables

Potatoes

Grains

Pastas

Beans

CALAVASITAS

Senator **Timothy Wirth**—*Colorado*

Spending a great deal of my time in Washington makes me miss Colorado and all it has to offer. One thing I always look forward to in Colorado is eating some good, spicy Mexican food. In between my trips home, I try to satisfy those urges to eat Mexican food by making calavasitas.

2	tablespoons butter or margarine
2	teaspoons red chili powder
2	teaspoons cumin
2 or 3	cloves garlic, diced or pressed
	freshly ground pepper to taste
2	large zucchini, diced
1	large onion, diced
4	ounces chopped green chilies
1	large tomato, diced
¾	cup Monterey Jack cheese, grated

Melt the butter or margarine in a heavy skillet. Add spices. Toss in the zucchini, onion, chilies, and diced tomato and sauté until the onions and zucchini are clear. Add the grated cheese and let it melt. Serve as a side dish or use the calavasitas in flour tortillas as a burro.

Makes 6 servings.

SPINACH AND ARTICHOKE BAKE

Representative **William Dannemeyer**—*California*

6 ounces marinated artichokes
20 ounces frozen spinach
8 ounces cream cheese, softened
2 tablespoons butter, softened
4 tablespoons milk
½ cup Parmesan cheese, grated

Cut artichokes and place in bottom of a 1-quart baking dish. Thaw spinach and drain. Spread spinach over artichokes. Blend cheese with butter and milk. Spread over spinach. Sprinkle with Parmesan cheese. Cover. Bake at 350° for 30 minutes. Remove the cover and bake for another 10 minutes.

Makes 6 servings.

BROCCOLI CASSEROLE

Representative **Thomas Carper**—*Delaware*

¼ cup onion, finely chopped
6 tablespoons margarine, divided
2 tablespoons flour
½ cup water
8 ounces Cheez Whiz
2 packages broccoli—chopped, thawed, and drained
3 eggs, well beaten
½ cup bread crumbs

In a large skillet, sauté onions in 4 tablespoons margarine. Add flour and water and cook on low heat until thick. Add Cheez Whiz and combine sauce and broccoli. Add eggs and mix gently until blended. Place mixture in a greased 1½-quart dish, cover with crumbs, and dot with rest of margarine. Bake at 325° for 30 minutes.

Makes 8 servings.

ZUCCHINI CASSEROLE

Representative **Ron Packard**—*California*

4 or 5 cups zucchini, grated
1¼ teaspoons salt
½ cup onion, chopped
¼ cup parsley, chopped
¼ cup Bisquick mix
4 eggs, beaten
pepper to taste
garlic powder to taste
bacon, crumbled

Sprinkle salt over zucchini and let stand for 1 hour. Then drain well. Fill 1½-quart baking dish with all ingredients. Stir to mix. Bake at 350° for 35 to 40 minutes.

Makes 10 to 12 servings.

FRENCH BEAN CASSEROLE

Senator **Spark Matsunaga**—*Hawaii*

> ½ cup margarine or butter
> ½ cup onions, chopped
> 8 ounces canned mushrooms, sliced
>   (reserve liquid)
> 5 ounces water chestnuts, thinly sliced
> ¼ cup margarine
> ⅓ cup flour
> 1 teaspoon salt
> ½ teaspoon pepper
> 1 cup milk
> ½ cup mushroom liquor
> 1 cup cheddar cheese, shredded
> 2 teaspoons soy sauce
> ⅛ teaspoon Tabasco sauce
> 20 ounces frozen French-cut green beans
> 1 can French-fried onions

In ½ cup margarine, sauté onions, mushrooms, and water chestnuts until tender. Set aside. Melt ¼ cup margarine and blend in flour, salt, and pepper. Gradually add milk and mushroom liquor. Stir until smooth and thickened. Add cheddar cheese, soy sauce, and Tabasco sauce. Stir until cheese melts.

In bottom of buttered 8 x 11-inch pan, layer half of the sautéed vegetables and green beans. Pour half of cheese sauce over vegetables. Repeat for second layer and top with remaining sauce. Bake at 350° for 15 minutes. Remove from oven and sprinkle crumbled onions on top. Return to oven and bake an additional 10 minutes.

Makes 8 servings.

SPINACH AND JALAPEÑO CHEESE

Senator **Albert Gore**—*Tennessee*

20 ounces frozen spinach, chopped
4 tablespoons butter
2 tablespoons flour
2 tablespoons onion, chopped
½ cup vegetable liquor (reserved spinach water)
½ cup evaporated milk
½ teaspoon black pepper
¾ teaspoon celery salt
¾ teaspoon garlic salt
 salt to taste
1 teaspoon Worcestershire sauce
 red pepper to taste
6 ounces jalapeño cheese

Cook spinach and drain, but reserve liquor. Melt butter, add flour, and stir. Blend until smooth. Add onions. Cool until soft, but not brown. Add vegetable liquor and milk, stirring constantly. Add seasonings and cut-up cheese. Stir until cheese is melted. Combine with spinach and serve hot.

Makes 8 servings.

ZUCCHINI AND CHERRY TOMATOES

Senator **Christopher Bond**—*Missouri*

A trip to the State Fair in Sedalia is an annual family ritual. Our son Sam loves the excitement of the midway, the children's barnyard, and the many agricultural and livestock displays. The giant zucchini are amazing, but the homegrown ones are fine in this tasty vegetable duo.

5 small zucchini
¼ cup butter
¼ cup onion, finely chopped
½ clove garlic, minced
¾ cup cherry tomatoes, halved
salt and freshly ground pepper
2 tablespoons sesame seeds, toasted
¼ cup parsley, finely chopped

Slice zucchini on the bias into ½-inch slices. In a 4-quart pan of rapidly boiling water, blanch zucchini for 1 minute. Rinse with cold water, drain, and pat dry.

Melt butter, add onion and garlic, and sauté until soft and golden brown. Add zucchini, cover, and cook for 2 minutes. Add tomatoes, cover, and cook for 1 minute. Season with salt and pepper. Add sesame seeds and parsley. Toss. Adjust seasonings to taste.

Makes 6 servings.

FRENCH-CUT STRING BEANS

Senator **Alfonse D'Amato**—*New York*

 1 **pound fresh string beans**
 ¼ **cup water**
 ¼ **cup corn oil**
 5 **tablespoons tomato sauce**
 1 **clove garlic, finely chopped**
 1 **teaspoon oregano**
 ¼ **cup Romano or Parmesan cheese, grated**
   salt and pepper

Wash string beans and drain. Cut beans French-style (lengthwise). Place sliced beans in heavy skillet. Add water, oil, tomato sauce, garlic, oregano, and grated cheese. Season with salt and pepper to taste. Cover skillet tightly and cook over low to medium heat for about 20 minutes, or until beans are slightly softened.

Makes 4 servings.

BEETS IN SOUR CREAM SAUCE

Representative **Philip Crane**—*Illinois*

¼ cup sour cream
1 tablespoon vinegar
1 teaspoon green onions, chopped
¾ teaspoon sugar
½ teaspoon salt
  dash of cayenne
2½ cups beets, cooked and drained

Combine first 6 ingredients in a saucepan. Add drained beets. Heat slowly and stir to coat each beet evenly. Do not boil.

Makes 6 to 8 servings.

COLESLAW

Senator **Christopher Bond**—*Missouri*

When Sam and I are lucky enough to fine the white bass running at the Lake of the Ozarks, our fish fry includes this tangy coleslaw, plus corn on the cob and sautéed zucchini.

12 ounces sour cream
6 tablespoons mayonnaise
3 tablespoons vinegar
4 tablespoons sugar
¼ teaspoon garlic salt
½ teaspoon salt
pepper to taste
1 large head cabbage
5 carrots, sliced
1 red pepper, seeded
1 green pepper, seeded
1 bunch green onions

Combine sour cream, mayonnaise, vinegar, sugar, garlic salt, salt, and pepper. Quarter cabbage and slice thinly. Do not cut too finely. Peel carrots and slice very thinly into rounds. Chop peppers and onions. Pour dressing mixture over cabbage, carrots, peppers, and onions. Toss and refrigerate.

Makes 12 servings.

DIJON VEGETABLES

Representative **Guy Vander Jagt**—*Michigan*

2 cups broccoli florets
2 cups cauliflowerets
2 cups small white onions
1 cup sharp cheddar cheese, grated
1 cup mayonnaise
3 tablespoons Dijon mustard
½ teaspoon salt
¼ teaspoon pepper
2 cloves garlic, crushed
1 teaspoon parsley

Steam vegetables individually. Combine vegetables and place half in a buttered glass casserole. Top with half the cheese. Repeat both layers. Combine remaining ingredients and pour over top. Bake at 350° for 30 minutes.

Makes 8 servings.

SOUFFLÉED CORN

Senator **Christopher Bond**—*Missouri*

Freshly picked corn is one of the treats of summer in MO.

6 ears corn
¾ cup butter, divided
½ cup sugar, divided
1 tablespoon flour
1½ teaspoons baking powder
½ cup evaporated milk
2 eggs, well beaten
1 teaspoon cinnamon

Preheat oven to 350°. Cut corn kernels from cobs. Melt ½ cup butter. Stir in ¼ cup of sugar. Gradually add flour and baking powder. Blend in milk and eggs, add corn. Mix well. Pour into a greased 8-inch, round baking dish. Bake 35 minutes or until done. Remove from oven. Melt remaining butter and combine with remaining sugar and the cinnamon. Brush top of soufflé with mixture while still hot.

Makes 6 to 8 servings.

ELLIE'S SOUR CREAM SCALLOPED CORN

Representative **Neal Smith**—*Iowa*

> ½ cup margarine, melted
> 14 ounces cream-style corn with liquid
> 12 ounces whole-kernel corn with liquid
> 2 eggs, beaten
> 1 cup sour cream
> 1 8-ounce box corn muffin mix

Combine margarine, corn, and eggs. Mix well. Stir in sour cream. Sprinkle muffin mix over mixture and beat well. Bake in 2½- to 3-quart casserole dish for 1 hour at 350°. May be frozen.

Makes 8 servings.

MARY'S SWEET POTATOES WITH CARAMEL SAUCE

Senator **James Sasser**—*Tennessee*

4 cups sweet potatoes—cooked, peeled, and mashed
¾ cup brown sugar
1 teaspoon vanilla
½ cup half-and-half
1 cup pecans

Sauce:

1 cup butter
1 cup sugar
½ cup half-and-half
pinch of salt
½ teaspoon vanilla

Cream potatoes and add sugar, vanilla, and half-and-half. Place in greased casserole. Make a well in the center and sprinkle with pecans. Bake at 350° until hot, about 15 minutes.

To make sauce, melt butter and sugar together in an iron skillet until golden. Slowly pour in half-and-half and cook for 2 minutes. Add salt and vanilla. Just before serving, pour sauce in the well. Serve hot.

LEMON YAM PUFF

Senator **Christopher Bond**—*Missouri*

This wintertime favorite has its origins in Ste. Genevieve County. French settlers founded the community prior to 1750. My ancestors were among the earliest to take up residence on the Missouri side of the Mississippi River. One member of the family was a member of the convention which framed the first Missouri constitution.

4 **pounds yams**
1 **cup brown sugar, packed**
½ **cup butter, softened**
½ **teaspoon salt**
2 **teaspoons orange rind, grated**
2 **teaspoons lemon rind, grated**

Preheat oven to 350°. Cook unpeeled, whole sweet potatoes in boiling water for 30 minutes or until tender. Drain, reserve liquid. Peel potatoes and mash until smooth. If mixture seems dry, add some reserved liquid. Add remaining ingredients and beat until light and fluffy. Transfer to a greased 2-quart casserole. Bake for 30 minutes and serve hot.

Makes 8 to 10 servings.

SWEET POTATOES

Representative **Wes Watkins**—*Oklahoma*

Always on the Watkins family table at Thanksgiving, Christmas, and Easter.

2 cups mashed sweet potatoes
½ cup butter, melted
1 cup brown sugar
2 eggs
¼ teaspoon nutmeg
¼ teaspoon cinnamon
¼ teaspoon cloves
1 cup evaporated milk
    miniature marshmallows or
    shredded coconut

Mix potatoes, butter, and sugar. Add eggs separately and beat after each. Add spices and milk. Mix thoroughly. Bake in buttered 9-inch, square glass baking pan for 35 minutes at 350°. When almost done, remove from oven. Sprinkle top with miniature marshmallows or shredded coconut. Return to oven and bake until done and topping is browned. May be frozen.

Makes 8 servings.

POTATO CASSEROLE

Representative **Dan Schaefer**—*Colorado*

32 ounces frozen hash brown potatoes
½ cup margarine
1 teaspoon salt
¼ teaspoon pepper
½ cup onions, chopped
1 10-ounce can cream of chicken soup
2 cups cheddar cheese, grated
2 cups sour cream

Topping:
¼ cup margarine, melted
2 cups cornflakes, crushed

Thaw potatoes and combine margarine, salt, pepper, onions, soup, cheese, and sour cream. Mix with the potatoes and pour in a 3-quart casserole dish. Melt margarine for topping and mix with cornflakes. Sprinkle topping over potato mixture. Bake for 45 minutes at 350°.

Note: Could be divided and frozen in serving amounts, then thawed and baked. When reheating, sprinkle top with a little water.

Makes 10 to 12 servings.

EASY IDAHO SPUDS

Representative **Richard Stallings**—*Idaho*

8 ounces cream cheese
1 10-ounce can cream of chicken soup
4 ounces sour cream
1 tablespoon onion, chopped
¾ package frozen hash brown potatoes
1 cup cheddar cheese, grated

Mix together first 3 ingredients in large saucepan. Add onion and hash browns. Heat thoroughly and stir until hash browns are broken up and mixed with the sauce. Place in a 2-quart casserole dish and top with cheddar cheese. Bake at 350° for 40 minutes, or until the cheese melts and the potatoes are hot.

Makes 6 servings.

BAKED RICE

Senator **Alfonse D'Amato**—*New York*

> 6 tablespoons butter
> 1 cup long-grain white rice
> 3 cups boiling water
> 4 chicken bouillon cubes
> ¼ cup Romano cheese, grated
> 1 green bell pepper, chopped
> 1 clove garlic, finely chopped
> freshly ground pepper to taste

Melt butter in heavy skillet and evenly brown uncooked rice. In casserole baking dish, dissolve bouillon cubes in boiling water. Stir until completely dissolved. Stir browned rice into casserole mixture. Add cheese, bell pepper, garlic, and pepper. Cover and place in 350° oven for 30 minutes.

Note: Sliced mushrooms may be added before baking.

Makes 4 servings.

RICE AND MUSHROOM CASSEROLE

Senator **Christopher Bond**—*Missouri*

My mother is a marvelous cook and introduced my wife to this dish after we were married. It is great with chicken, game, or pork.

2 cups onion, sliced
2 cups fresh mushrooms, sliced
½ cup butter
1 cup beef consommé
1 cup water
1 cup uncooked rice
    salt and freshly ground pepper

Preheat oven to 350°. Sauté onions and mushrooms in butter. Add consommé and water. Mix in rice and season with salt and pepper. Transfer to a buttered, 2-quart casserole. Bake covered for 45 minutes, or until done. Garnish with snipped chives.

Makes 6 servings.

RICE-NOODLE CASSEROLE

Senator **Howard Metzenbaum**—*Ohio*

> 8 ounces fine noodles
> ½ pound margarine
> 2 cups Minute Rice
> 2 tablespoons soy sauce
> 1 cup chicken bouillon
> 2½ cups chicken broth
> 2 cups onion soup
> ¼ cup slivered almonds

Brown raw noodles in margarine. Mix in rest of ingredients and transfer to casserole dish. Bake at 350° uncovered for 45 minutes. Stir often to prevent sticking.

Makes 8 to 10 servings.

RICE AND BROCCOLI CASSEROLE

Senator **James Exon**—*Nebraska*

10 ounces frozen broccoli, cut up
1 onion, chopped fine
1 tablespoon vegetable oil
1 10-ounce can cream of chicken soup
½ cup Cheez Whiz
½ cup milk
1 teaspoon salt
1 cup Minute Rice, uncooked

Thaw broccoli. Combine onion and oil in saucepan and heat. Add broccoli and cook for 5 minutes. Add soup and heat to boiling. Stir constantly and reduce heat. Add Cheez Whiz and milk. Add salt and cook for a few more minutes. Add rice and stir. Pour into lightly buttered 1½-quart casserole dish, cover, and bake for 30 minutes at 350°.

Note: Garnish with sautéed mushrooms before baking, if desired.

Makes 6 servings.

CHEESE GRITS I

Representative **Beverly Byron**—*Maryland*

> **1 cup quick-cooking grits**
> **2 cups sharp cheese, shredded**
> **½ cup butter**
> **2 eggs, beaten**
> **2 cloves garlic, minced**

Cook grits as directed on package. Stir in cheese, butter, eggs, and garlic. Cook over low heat for 5 minutes. Pour into a 2-quart, greased casserole dish. Bake at 350° for 45 minutes.

Makes 6 servings.

Editor's note: Grits are a Southern tradition served usually at breakfast, or at any time of the day. Additions such as cheese and garlic liven up the flavor.

CHEESE GRITS II

Senator **Terry Sanford**—*North Carolina*

> 4 cups boiling water
> 1 cup quick-cooking grits
> ¼ cup butter or margarine
> 6 ounces cheddar cheese
> 2 eggs
> ¾ cup milk

Bring water to boil and slowly add the grits. Stir constantly until done, about 3 to 5 minutes. Remove from heat. Stir in butter and cheese and thoroughly melt. Separate eggs. Place egg yolks in measuring cup and fill with milk to make 1 cup. Beat egg whites until peaked and fold in lightly. Pour into greased casserole dish. Bake at 375° for 30 minutes.

Makes 6 servings.

ARIZONA BAKED BEANS

Senator **John McCain**—*Arizona*

This dish is a favorite with barbecued foods.

1 medium onion, chopped
1 teaspoon butter
16 ounces red kidney beans
16 ounces B&M baked beans
1 cup catsup
1 cup brown sugar, packed
1 tablespoon vinegar
1 teaspoon yellow mustard
4 strips fried bacon, cooled and crumbled

In a skillet, sauté chopped onion with a teaspoon of butter. In a large baking pot combine kidney beans, B&M baked beans, catsup, brown sugar, vinegar, mustard, and bacon. After combining and stirring enough to mix the ingredients, add the sautéed onion. Mix well. Bake in a covered dish at 350° for 35 minutes or until piping hot.

Makes 10 servings.

Main Dishes

Casseroles

Soufflés

Savory Pies

Sandwiches

BREAKFAST SAUSAGE CASSEROLE

Representative **Tom Coleman**—*Missouri*

8 **eggs, slightly beaten**
1 **cup milk**
6 **slices white bread, cubed**
1 **cup cheddar cheese, grated**
1 **pound sausage—browned, crumbled, and drained**
1 **teaspoon dry mustard**
   parsley

Mix all ingredients and sprinkle with parsley. Refrigerate overnight. Bake in a 9 x 12-inch glass pan at 350° for 45 minutes.

Makes 8 to 10 servings.

CHICKEN AND
BROCCOLI CASSEROLE

Senator **William Armstrong**—*Colorado*

20 ounces frozen broccoli spears
1 cup mayonnaise
1 tablespoon lemon juice
2 cans cream of chicken soup
1½ teaspoons curry powder
4 large chicken breasts—cooked, boned,
    and diced
½ cup sharp cheddar cheese, shredded

Cook broccoli as directed and place in bottom of baking dish. Mix mayonnaise, lemon juice, chicken soup, and curry powder together. Fold in diced chicken. Pour over broccoli. Bake for 30 to 40 minutes at 350°. Top with cheese, if desired, during last 10 minutes of baking.

Makes 10 servings.

EXTRA-MEATY LASAGNA

Senator **Kent Conrad**—*North Dakota*

This is a great main meal just for the family or for dinner guests. The only other dish you need with it is a tossed salad to make a complete meal. We use prepared tomato sauce because it's so good and saves time.

1½ pounds extra-lean ground beef
1 medium onion, chopped
1 pound sweet Italian sausage links
16 ounces seasoned, meaty tomato sauce
1 teaspoon oregano
1 teaspoon ground black pepper
1 teaspoon garlic powder
   dash of salt
¼ cup vegetable or olive oil
8 ounces lasagna noodles
3 cups low-fat creamed cottage cheese
2 tablespoons dried parsley flakes
1 egg, beaten
1 pound mozzarella cheese, shredded
1 cup grated Parmesan cheese

Brown ground beef and onion. Add a small amount of oil to moisten, if necessary. Remove ground beef and onion. Retain fat in pan and add sausage links. Brown on all sides. In saucepan place tomato sauce, oregano, pepper, and garlic powder. Add ground beef and onion, mixing well. Simmer. Drain fat from sausage, pat with towel to remove excess oil and fat. Place sausage in saucepan with tomato sauce and meat mixture, continue simmering. DO NOT BOIL. Stir often.

Bring 3 quarts water, dash of salt, and oil to boil in large pot. Add noodles, one at a time. Bring to a second boil, then follow cooking directions on lasagna package. While noodles are cooking, mix cottage cheese, parsley, and beaten egg in a bowl. Set aside. Remove sausage from sauce and cut into ¼-inch round slices. Stir sauce to avoid sticking. After sauce has cooked for 15 minutes (or until sausage is cooked thoroughly), remove from heat.

Drain noodles. Layer one half of the noodles in a lightly greased 13 x 9 x 2-inch baking dish spread with half of the cottage cheese mixture. Add half of the sausage slices, half of the sauce and meat mixture; sprinkle half of the shredded or sliced mozzarella cheese. Repeat layers. Sprinkle Parmesan cheese on top. Bake for 30 to 35 minutes at 375°.

Note: This recipe can be prepared in advance and refrigerated. Bake for 45 minutes to 1 hour. Wait a few minutes after baking, then slice and serve.

Makes 10 servings.

BEEF STROGANOFF

Senator **Robert Byrd**—*West Virginia*

1½ **pounds round steak**
¼ **cup butter**
1 **cup mushrooms, sliced**
1 **clove garlic, minced**
½ **cup chopped onion**
1¼ **cups tomato soup**
1 **cup sour cream**
salt
pepper

Cut beef into long thin strips. Brown well in butter in a heavy skillet. Add mushrooms, garlic, and onion. Cook until lightly browned. Blend in tomato soup, sour cream, salt, and pepper. Cover and simmer about 1 hour, or until beef is tender. Stir occasionally. Serve with hot cooked rice.

Makes 6 servings.

BEEF SUKIYAKI

Senator **Spark Matsunaga**—*Hawaii*

> 1 large onion, sliced
> 6 mushrooms, sliced
> beef suet
> 6½ ounces bamboo shoots, sliced
> 1 package yam noodles
> ¼ cup mirin (rice wine)
> ½ cup soy sauce
> ¼ cup water
> ⅓ cup sugar
> 1 block tofu, cubed
> 2 won bok leaves, cut in 1-inch pieces
> 1 pound New York cut beef, thinly sliced
> 2 scallions, cut in 1-inch lengths

In a large skillet, sauté onions and mushrooms in suet. Add bamboo shoots, yam noodles, and mirin. Mix well. Combine soy sauce, water, and sugar and add to mixture until it bubbles. Add tofu, won bok, beef, and scallions in that order, turning beef over until it cooks.

Note: Tofu must be handled gently or it will not retain its shape. Do not overcook beef.

Makes 6 servings.

SAUCY SEAFOOD CASSEROLE

Representative **Tom Sawyer**—*Ohio*

1 cup mayonnaise
½ cup chili sauce
½ teaspoon chutney
½ teaspoon Escoffier Diablo Sauce
1 teaspoon Worcestershire sauce
½ teaspoon paprika
few grains cayenne pepper
14 ounces crabmeat or lobster, or 1 pound shrimp (cooked)
Parmesan cheese
3 tablespoons butter

Mix all ingredients except seafood together. Taste and add more of the above seasoning as desired. Place seafood in a 1-quart casserole. Cover with sauce. Sprinkle with a little Parmesan cheese and about 3 tablespoons of melted butter. Bake at 350° until nicely browned, approximately 30 minutes. Serve on or with buttered toast points.

Makes 6 servings.

MEXICAN MOUND

President **George Bush**

Barbara serves this dish in the kitchen for a warm and hearty meal. The ingredients are easy to keep in the house. Children or guests can all help with chopping and grating. It's fun!!

2 pounds ground meat
1 package taco seasoning mix
1 package corn chips
1 cup cheddar cheese, grated
1 small onion, chopped
10 ripe black olives, chopped
1 tomato, chopped
1 cup sour cream
1 cup lettuce, shredded
1 medium can frozen avocado dip, thawed

Follow instructions on taco seasoning mix for browning meat. Serve meat from a big pot simmering on the stove. Fill individual bowls with each of the ingredients. Start with a mound of corn chips, a spoon of piping hot meat, cheese, etc.

KIKA'S TEXAS PICADILLO

Representative **Kika de la Garza**—*Texas*

This is very good served with refried beans or as a filling for tacos (corn tortillas) or burritos (flour tortillas).

2 **pounds lean ground beef**
2 **large cloves garlic, mashed**
2 **large onions, diced**
2 **cups canned tomatoes, chopped**
2 **medium potatoes, cubed**
½ **teaspoon cumin**
½ **teaspoon pepper**
1 **tablespoon cilantro**

Sauté beef, garlic, and onions in frying pan over medium heat until meat is brown. Drain excess fat. Mix in all other ingredients and cook covered over medium-low heat for 20 or 25 minutes, stirring occasionally. Suitable for freezing.

Makes 4 servings.

GREEK SPAGHETTI

Representative **Peter Smith**—*Vermont*

    2 medium onions, chopped
    1½ pounds ground lamb
    28 ounces crushed tomatoes
    ¼ teaspoon cinnamon
       salt and pepper
    ¾ cup grated Parmesan cheese
    1 pound spaghetti

Brown onions and add lamb. Cook until pink color is
gone. Add tomatoes and seasonings and simmer for
30 minutes. Add cheese. Pour over cooked spaghetti.

Makes 6 servings.

SEAFOOD CASSEROLE

Representative **William Hughes**—*New Jersey*

> 1 cup celery, chopped
> 1 cup green pepper, chopped
> ⅓ cup onion, chopped
> ¼ teaspoon Worcestershire sauce
> ½ to ¾ cup mayonnaise
> 1 pound slightly cooked shrimp, cut in halves
> 1 pound slightly cooked scallops, cut in halves
> 1 pound crab legs
> sherry to taste
> buttered bread crumbs

Combine first 8 ingredients. Add sherry and spread in baking dish. Top with crumbs. Bake at 350° for 30 to 40 minutes. Serve with wild rice.

Makes 10 to 12 servings.

CRAB AND SHRIMP CASSEROLE

Senator **William Armstrong**—*Colorado*

 1 medium green pepper, chopped
 1 medium onion, chopped
 1 cup celery, chopped
13 ounces canned white crabmeat—drained, rinsed, and flaked
13 ounces canned shrimp, drained and rinsed
 ½ teaspoon salt
 ⅛ teaspoon pepper
 1 teaspoon Worcestershire sauce
 1 cup mayonnaise
 1 cup buttered crumbs or crumbled Triscuits

Mix all ingredients together except crumbs. Place in a casserole. Sprinkle with buttered crumbs. Bake at 350° for 30 minutes. Also delicious the next day served cold.

Makes 6 servings.

HAM MOUSSE

Senator **Christopher Bond**—*Missouri*

During a July 4th trip to Hannibal for the annual Tom Sawyer Days, we were treated to this deliciously simple ham mousse served with a spicy homemade mustard. The events highlighted are the Tom Sawyer and Becky Thatcher look-alike contest and the fence-painting contest on the banks of the Mississippi River.

4 cups ground cooked ham
1 large onion, diced
½ cup golden raisins
2 to 3 tablespoons dry sherry
1 teaspoon prepared horseradish
½ teaspoon nutmeg
2 teaspoons Dijon mustard
2 tablespoons unflavored gelatin
2 tablespoons cold water
1 cup chicken stock
1 cup heavy cream, whipped
2 tablespoons parsley, finely chopped

Combine ham, onion, and raisins in a food processor. Puree, or put through the finest blade of a meat grinder three times. Combine meat mixture, sherry, horseradish, nutmeg, and mustard. Set aside.

Soften gelatin in cold water for 5 minutes. Bring chicken stock to a boil, add gelatin, and stir over medium heat until dissolved. Add to ham mixture, blend thoroughly. Cool 10 to 15 minutes. Fold whipped cream and parsley into mixture. Turn into a well-oiled 5-cup mold. Chill 3 hours, or until firm. Unmold on a plate garnished with sweet gherkins or stuffed green olives. Serve with very thin slices of French or rye bread.

Note: Because of its richness, serve the mousse in small portions when using as an entree.

Makes 16 to 20 servings.

CHEESE SOUFFLÉ

Senator **Chuck Grassley**—*Iowa*

*From Nan, whose husband is
in the Navy.*

8 slices day-old bread, crusts trimmed
8 slices Old English cheese
diced ham or cooked chicken (optional)
Mix:
  6 eggs, well beaten
  3 cups milk
  ½ teaspoon salt
  ½ teaspoon dry mustard

Lay bread in bottom of buttered 9 x 13-inch pan.
Top with cheese. Pour well-mixed egg mixture over.
Cover and refrigerate overnight. Before baking, top
with crushed cornflakes mixed with melted butter.
(If you use meat, put it under the cheese.) Bake for 1
hour at 350°. Serve while hot.

Makes 10 servings.

EGGS RIO GRANDE

Representative **Kika de la Garza**—*Texas*

> **2** tablespoons oil or butter
> ½ cup fresh tomato, diced
> ½ cup green pepper, diced
> **1** small onion, diced
> **6** eggs
>   salt and pepper
>   jalapeño pepper or Tabasco sauce
>   (optional)

In a skillet, sauté tomato, green pepper, and onion in oil or butter until tender. Add eggs, letting them simmer on top until they turn a little white. Stir the whole mixture, and continue stirring until eggs are done. Add salt and pepper to taste, and jalapeño pepper or Tabasco if desired.

Makes 4 servings.

LANGOSTINO SOUFFLÉ

Representative **Robert Smith**—*New Hampshire*

An elegant one-dish supper for company. It is great for a buffet with a salad and crusty bread.

2 tablespoons onion, finely chopped
2 tablespoons green or red pepper, finely chopped
1 tablespoon butter
1 12-ounce package frozen langostinos
½ pound American cheese, cubed
⅓ teaspoon dry mustard
¼ teaspoon salt
3 eggs, beaten
2 cups milk
⅓ cup melted butter
6 slices bread, cubed

Sauté onion and pepper in 1 tablespoon butter. Mix all ingredients together. Let stand in refrigerator overnight. Bake at 350° for 1 hour.

Makes 8 servings.

Representative **Ralph Regula**—*Ohio*

9 slices white bread, crusts removed
4 cups cooked chicken, cubed
1 tablespoon margarine
8 ounces sliced mushrooms, drained
6 ounces water chestnuts
9 slices sharp cheddar cheese
½ cup mayonnaise
4 eggs, well beaten
2 cups milk
1 teaspoon salt
1 can cream of mushroom soup, undiluted
1 can cream of celery soup, undiluted
2 ounces pimento, drained and chopped
2 cups buttered, coarse bread crumbs

Line a buttered 13 x 9 x 2-inch baking dish with bread. Top with chicken. Sauté mushrooms in margarine and spoon over chicken. Top with water chestnuts and cheese. Combine mayonnaise, eggs, milk, and salt. Beat well. Pour over cheese. Combine soups and pimento, stirring well. Spoon over casserole. Cover with aluminum foil and refrigerate about 8 hours or overnight. Bake uncovered at 350° for 30 minutes. Remove from oven. Top with bread crumbs. Return to oven and bake an additional 15 to 20 minutes or until set.

Makes 8 servings.

ASPARAGUS CHEESE PIE

Senator **Steve Symms**—*Idaho*

3 pounds fresh asparagus, cut in 1-inch
   pieces
salt and pepper
nutmeg to taste
1 unbaked deep-dish pie shell
¾ cup grated Swiss cheese
1 cup shredded or ground ham
4 eggs, well beaten
6 tablespoons grated Romano cheese

Steam asparagus until just tender. Season with salt, pepper, and nutmeg. Arrange asparagus in pie shell. Sprinkle with Swiss cheese and ham. Pour eggs over all. Top with Romano cheese. Bake at 350° for 30 to 40 minutes, or until firm. Let set for 10 minutes before cutting. May be frozen.

Makes 6 to 8 servings.

BIEROCH

Senator **Robert Dole**—*Kansas*

> 1 medium onion, finely chopped
>   butter
> 1 pound ground beef
> 1 medium cabbage, shredded
>   salt and pepper to taste
> 1 recipe your favorite yeast dough

Brown onion in butter in skillet. Add ground beef and brown. Steam cabbage in separate pan in butter just until done. Add cabbage to beef mixture. Season with salt and pepper.

Roll dough out to ¼-inch thickness. Cut into 6-inch squares. Place 3 tablespoons beef mixture into each square. Pull 4 corners together, pinch edges firmly. Place in greased pan, pinched edges down. Bake at 350° for 30 minutes or until done. Serve hot. Bieroch may be wrapped in foil and frozen.

Makes 6 servings.

TAILGATE HERO SANDWICH

Senator **Christopher Bond**—*Missouri*

Mizzou football has always been a family affair for the Bonds. This colossal sandwich which serves a crowd is our standby for Tiger tailgates. Kit's dad, Art Bond, who rarely missed a home game, was captain of the 1924 team which won the Missouri Valley Championship, defeating Big Ten winner Chicago.

1 **crusty loaf French bread**
prepared Italian dressing
mayonnaise
Durkee's hot sauce
⅓ **pound each: smoked turkey, corned beef, ham**
⅓ **pound each: baby Swiss, provolone, New York cheddar cheese, thinly sliced**
2 **medium tomatoes, thinly sliced and drained**
2 **medium green peppers, thinly sliced into rings**
1 **red onion, thinly sliced and separated into rings**

Cut bread loaf in half lengthwise. Scoop out centers, leaving a ½-inch shell. Spread both halves with Italian dressing. Generously spread mayonnaise over one half and Durkee sauce over the other. Layer turkey, corned beef, and ham on both halves. Layer cheeses on meat, and tomatoes, green peppers, and onion on cheeses. Carefully put halves together. Wrap sandwich tightly with foil and refrigerate. To serve, cut in 2-inch slices. The sandwich may be prepared and refrigerated for up to 48 hours before serving.

Makes 12 to 16 servings.

OPEN-FACE IDAHO
APPLE SANDWICH

Senator **Steve Symms**—*Idaho*

This is a way to give an old sandwich favorite, ham and cheese, a new look and a distinctive new flavor. It tastes just as good as it looks, and is perfect for entertaining.

     6 slices white or wheat bread
       mayonnaise
       mustard
     6 slices cooked ham
3 or 4 Red or Golden Delicious apples
   12 slices (1 ounce each) American cheese

Spread bread with mayonnaise, then with mustard. Top with ham slices. Core apples, but do not peel. Slice crosswise about ⅛ inch thick to make 18 slices. Place 3 apple slices on each sandwich. Top with two cheese slices. Broil under medium heat until cheese melts and browns slightly. Serve at once.

Makes 6 open-face sandwiches.

CALIFORNIAN

Representative **Lee Hamilton**—*Indiana*

Our favorite sandwich is a Californian, and it is our Sunday evening regular. Other vegetables can be added if desired, but we like this combo.

4 slices whole-grain bread
mayonnaise
tomato, thinly sliced
avocado, thinly sliced
sweet onion, thinly sliced
Jarlsberg cheese, thinly sliced
salt and pepper to taste

Assemble ingredients to serve as 4 open-faced sandwiches.

Meats

Beef

Moose

Pork

Ham

Lamb

MARINADE FOR
FLANK STEAK

Senator **Bob Packwood**—*Oregon*

      flank steak
½ **cup red wine**
½ **cup soy sauce**
½ **cup water**
½ **teaspoon ginger**
½ **teaspoon garlic powder**
1 **teaspoon brown sugar**
1 **teaspoon lemon juice**

Slice flank steak diagonally across the grain into strips 1 inch wide. Marinate 2 hours minimum in other ingredients. Broil or grill for about 5 minutes on each side.

LITE-AND-LEAN
BEEF BROIL

Representative **Larry Craig**—*Idaho*

    1½ **pounds sirloin, top round, or flank steak**
    ½ **cup soy sauce**
    ¼ **cup water**
    2 **tablespoons lemon juice**
    2 **tablespoons honey**
    1 **teaspoon instant minced onion**
    ¼ **teaspoon garlic powder**

Combine marinade ingredients in a nonmetal pan. Add beef and turn to coat. Marinate beef for 24 to 48 hours in refrigerator. Broil beef to desired doneness (do not overcook; best served medium-rare). To serve, slice beef across the grain into thin slices. Sprinkle with sesame seeds.

Makes 4 to 6 servings.

CABBAGE ROLLS

Senator **Robert Byrd**—*West Virginia*

1 pound lean ground beef
1 cup cooked rice
1 small onion, chopped
1 teaspoon salt
¼ teaspoon pepper
1 egg
   cabbage leaves
16 ounces tomato sauce
¼ cup water

Mix ground beef, cooked rice, chopped onion, salt, pepper, and egg together. Trim off thickest part of stem from cabbage leaves. Blanch leaves to soften. Divide meat into 6 equal portions, wrap in a leaf, and fasten with wooden picks. Brown cabbage rolls slightly in oil. Add the tomato sauce and ¼ cup water. Cover and cook slowly about 40 minutes.

Makes 6 servings.

BBQ ROAST BEEF

Representative **Gerry Sikorski**—*Minnesota*

4 pounds beef roast
2 tablespoons salt
¼ teaspoon pepper
½ cup water
¼ teaspoon paprika
½ teaspoon dry mustard
¼ cup lemon juice
¼ cup catsup
1 tablespoon Worcestershire sauce
1 onion, chopped
2 garlic cloves, minced
2 tablespoons brown sugar
2 drops Tabasco
8 ounces tomato sauce

Combine all of the above and simmer covered for 6 hours. Pick out bones and serve on buns.

Makes 12 servings.

PEPPERED RIB EYE
OF BEEF

Representative **Gerry Sikorski**—*Minnesota*

5- to 8-pound boneless rib eye roast
½ cup coarsely cracked pepper
½ teaspoon ground cardamom
1 tablespoon tomato paste
1 teaspoon paprika
¾ cup red wine vinegar
½ teaspoon garlic powder
1 cup soy sauce
Gravy:
  water
1½ teaspoons cornstarch

Trim fat from roast. Combine pepper and cardamom and rub over roast, pressing in with palm of hand. Place roast in shallow pan. Pour over this a mixture of next 5 ingredients. Marinate overnight in refrigerator.

Remove meat from marinade and let stand for 1 hour at room temperature. Wrap meat in foil, place in shallow pan and bake at 300° for 2 hours, or until medium rare. Open foil, ladle out and reserve drippings. Brown roast at 350° uncovered while making gravy: to 1 cup meat juice, add 1 cup water. Strain drippings and remove fat. If desired, add cornstarch for gravy.

Makes 10 to 16 servings.

GRILLED BRISKET
OF BEEF

Representative **Clay Shaw**—*Florida*

　1　brisket of beef
　　　Adolph's meat tenderizer
　　　ground pepper
　　　Lawry's seasoning salt
　　　garlic salt (or garlic powder)
Barbecue sauce:
　1　cup tomato juice
　1　large onion, chopped
　2　tablespoons vinegar
　1　small bottle Worcestershire sauce
　　　juice of 1 lemon
　　　salt and pepper to taste
　1　clove garlic, crushed
　1　can beer
　20　ounces tomato puree
　　　Lawry's seasoning salt, to taste

The night before, season beef with Adolph's
tenderizer. The next day, season with pepper,
Lawry's salt, and garlic salt or garlic powder.

Cook over charcoal fat side up for 3½ to 4 hours.
Add barbecue sauce and cook an additional 30 to 40
minutes. Let stand or wrap in foil. Slice very thin.

For barbecue sauce, mix together in saucepan the
tomato juice, onion, vinegar, Worcestershire sauce,
lemon juice, salt and pepper, and garlic. Simmer for
1 hour. Add the beer, tomato puree, and Lawry's
salt and simmer for another 30 minutes.

SWEDISH MEATBALLS

Senator **Dan Coats**—*Indiana*

Dan's mother was born in Sweden and this is a family recipe. Vera Swanlund Coats passed this recipe on to Marcia Coats. It is a Coats family traditional Christmas dish.

¾ **pound lean ground beef**
½ **pound ground veal**
¼ **pound ground pork**
1½ **cups soft bread crumbs**
1 **cup light cream**
½ **cup chopped onion**
3 **tablespoons butter, divided**
1 **egg**
¼ **cup finely chopped parsley**
1½ **teaspoon salt**
¼ **teaspoon ginger**
⅛ **teaspoon pepper**
⅛ **teaspoon nutmeg**
Gravy:
2 **tablespoons all-purpose flour**
1 **cup light cream**
½ **teaspoon instant coffee**

Have meat ground together twice. Soak bread crumbs in cream for 5 minutes. Cook onion in 1 tablespoon butter until tender. Mix meats, crumb mixture, onion, egg, parsley, and seasonings. Beat vigorously until fluffy (5 minutes on medium speed or 8 minutes by hand). Form in 1½-inch balls. Brown lightly in 2 tablespoons butter, shaking skillet to keep balls round. Remove balls. Reserve drippings.

To make gravy, stir flour into drippings in skillet. Add light cream and coffee. Heat and stir until gravy thickens. Return balls to gravy, cover, cook slowly about 30 minutes, basting occasionally.

Makes 3 dozen 1½-inch balls.

BEEF IN BEER

Representative **Lynn Martin**—*Illinois*

I like to serve it over rice or noodles. Wonderful!

½ cup flour
1½ pounds stew beef
½ cup margarine or butter, divided
2 tablespoons red wine vinegar
2 cans beer
½ teaspoon thyme
¼ cup parsley flakes
3 large onions, sliced
dash salt
pinch sugar

Dredge beef in flour and brown in ¼ cup of the margarine (a cast-iron Dutch oven using high heat browns meat quickly). Add wine vinegar to deglaze pan. Gradually add beer to cover beef. The flour thickens the beer. Add spices and bake for 45 minutes at 350°. In saucepan, use remaining butter, adding salt and sugar, to cook onions until soft. Once soft, add onions to beef and beer mixture. Cook an additional 15 to 30 minutes.

Makes 6 servings.

QUICK-AND-EASY
TACO MEATBALLS

Senator **Conrad Burns**—*Montana*

This is a great and easy dish.

2 **pounds hamburger**
½ **onion, chopped**
2 **eggs, slightly beaten**
1 **package taco mix**
   salt and pepper
   garlic salt to taste

Mix ingredients together. Form into small meatballs and place on cookie sheet. Bake at 400° for 15 minutes.

Makes 6 to 8 servings.

MOOSE SWISS STEAK

Representative **Don Young**—*Alaska*

This is a good recipe to represent my state, because many Alaskan residents are able to enjoy fresh moose meat.

3 pounds moose steak
2 tablespoons lemon juice
¼ cup flour
1 teaspoon dry mustard
1½ teaspoons salt
¼ teaspoon pepper
shortening
1 small onion, sliced
14½ ounces canned tomatoes

Sprinkle meat with lemon juice and pierce with fork to tenderize. Mix dry ingredients together and roll meat in mixture. Brown slowly in about ⅓ to ½ cup shortening. Place in a casserole dish and cover with sliced onions and tomatoes. Bake at 325° for 1½ to 2 hours.

Makes 6 servings.

IOWA CHOPS

Senator **Tom Harkin**—*Iowa*

2 Iowa pork chops

Stuffing:
- **½ cup whole-kernel corn**
- **½ cup bread crumbs**
- **pinch of salt**
- **pinch of pepper**
- **¾ tablespoon parsley**
- **pinch of sage**
- **½ tablespoon onion, chopped**
- **½ cup apple, diced**
- **1 tablespoon whole milk**

Basting sauce:
- **¼ cup mustard**
- **¼ cup honey**
- **½ teaspoon salt**
- **¼ teaspoon rosemary leaves**
- **pinch of pepper**

Cut pocket into side of chops. Combine stuffing ingredients and stuff chops. Brown in pan, then bake at 350° for about 1 hour. Baste often with basting sauce mixture.

Makes 2 servings.

MANDARIN PORK STEAKS

Senator **Christopher Bond**—*Missouri*

Any backyard chef will be proud to serve this Joplin dish.

1 beef bouillon cube
⅓ cup hot water
1 teaspoon ground ginger
2 teaspoons salt
1 tablespoon sugar
¼ cup honey
¼ cup soy sauce
4 to 6 pork arm or blade steaks

Place bouillon and water in a large glass, stainless steel, or enamelware pan. Stir until dissolved. Add all ingredients except pork. Mix well. Add pork. Refrigerate at least 2 hours, preferably overnight, turning occasionally.

Preheat oven to 350° or prepare outdoor grill. Remove steaks from marinade and place on rack in shallow roasting pan. Bake for 50 minutes or until done, or grill 4 inches from coals 12 to 15 minutes on each side, or until juices run clear. Baste each side frequently with marinade.

Makes 4 to 6 servings.

PEPPER PORK CHOPS

Senator **Alfonse D'Amato**—*New York*

> 2 medium potatoes
> 4 tablespoons corn oil
> 6 medium pork chops
> 3 green bell peppers, sliced
> 3 to 4 vinegar peppers
> ¼ cup vinegar from pepper jar
> salt and pepper

Peel and cube potatoes. Boil until slightly tender. In a heavy skillet, add corn oil and pork chops to brown. Remove pork chops after browning and add sliced bell peppers. Cook peppers until slightly tender. Add pork chops and potatoes and cook for 5 minutes. Add sliced vinegar peppers and vinegar to skillet mixture. Cover and let cook over medium heat for 5 to 10 minutes. Salt and pepper to taste.

Makes 4 servings.

TENNESSEE COUNTRY HAM

Senator **James Sasser**—*Tennessee*

country ham
bread crumbs
apple cider
brown sugar

Put ham in lard stand and totally cover with water. Boil 1½ minutes per pound. Place top on lard stand and remove from stove. Wrap stand in old newspapers and old blanket, or even an old piece of carpeting or old overcoat. Allow to remain wrapped for 20 to 22 hours.

Skin the ham. When cool, take to your butcher and ask him to debone it and grind all lean scraps from the trimming and deboning. Then combine equal parts of ground ham, bread crumbs, apple cider and brown sugar. This makes a stuffing to go back into the cavity left by deboning and should be the consistency of turkey stuffing. Place stuffed ham back into oven and bake at 300° for 30 to 40 minutes.

BAKED IDAHO
APPLE 'N LAMB CHOPS

Senator **Steve Symms**—*Idaho*

When you want to impress your family or guests, put this dish on the table. Although it's easy to prepare, no one will believe it. The apples and molasses add a distinctive taste to the subtle flavor of the lamb.

6 **Idaho loin lamb chops, 1 inch thick**
½ **teaspoon salt**
3 **large Idaho Rome or Red Delicious apples**
5 **tablespoons flour**
3 **tablespoons molasses**
2 **cups hot water**
1 **tablespoon cider vinegar**
⅓ **cup golden raisins**
12 **maraschino cherries**

Score fat edges of chops. Brown fat edges in frying pan, then brown chops on both sides. Arrange in shallow baking dish. Sprinkle with salt. Core apples, but do not peel. Cut into thick rings and place on chops. Add flour to fat in frying pan and stir until browned.

Combine molasses and water, add to frying pan. Stir over low heat until mixture thickens. Add vinegar and raisins. Pour over chops and apples. Cover. Bake at 350° for 1 hour. Add maraschino cherries.

Makes 6 servings.

GRILLED BEEF TENDERLOIN

Representative **James Sensenbrenner**—*Wisconsin*

¾ **cup soy sauce**
¼ **cup oil**
¼ **cup flour**
½ **cup sugar**
½ **cup toasted sesame seeds**
2 **green onions, sliced**
2 **cloves garlic, mashed**
¼ **teaspoon pepper**
4 **pounds beef tenderloin, sliced in filets**

Combine all ingredients except meat. Marinate filets in mixture at least ½ hour before grilling. Grill filets to desired doneness, using mixture to baste. Any remaining filets may be frozen in marinade.

Makes 6 servings.

Poultry and Seafood

Chicken

Cornish Hens

Duck

Shellfish

Fish

CHICKEN CACCIATORE I

Representative **Don Sundquist**—*Tennessee*

My wife enjoys cooking this dish, because it is so easy to prepare and can be fixed ahead of time. It is also one of my favorites.

¼ cup all-purpose flour
½ teaspoon salt
2½- to 3-pound broiler-fryer chicken, cut up
¼ cup olive oil
½ cup onion, chopped
¼ cup celery, chopped
¼ cup green pepper, chopped
2 cloves garlic, minced
1 16-ounce can tomatoes, cut up
8 ounces tomato sauce
3 ounces sliced mushrooms, drained
⅓ cup dry white wine
1 teaspoon salt
½ teaspoon dried basil, crushed
½ teaspoon dried rosemary, crushed
pepper to taste

Combine flour and salt in a clear plastic bag or paper bag. Add a few pieces of chicken at a time and shake. In an ovenproof skillet brown the chicken in hot olive oil and remove chicken. In same skillet cook onion, celery, green pepper, and garlic until tender, but not brown.

Return chicken to skillet. Combine tomatoes, tomato sauce, mushrooms, wine, salt, basil, rosemary, and pepper. Pour over chicken. Cover and bake at 350° until chicken is tender, about 1 hour. Remove the chicken to warm serving dish. Ladle sauce over top.

Makes 4 servings.

CRUNCHY SESAME CHICKEN

Senator **Alan Cranston**—*California*

> ½ **cup soy sauce**
> 2 **tablespoons vegetable oil**
> 1 **clove garlic, diced**
> 1 **cut-up fryer chicken, 3 to 4 pounds**
> ½ **cup bread crumbs**
> ⅓ **cup wheat germ**
> 2 **tablespoons chopped parsley**
> 2½ **tablespoons sesame seeds**
> ¾ **teaspoon pepper**
> ½ **teaspoon paprika**

Mix soy sauce, oil, and garlic clove in bowl. Pour over chicken in a shallow pan. Let marinate for 15 minutes covering both sides of chicken.

In pie pan, mix bread crumbs, wheat germ, parsley, sesame seeds, pepper, and paprika. Remove chicken from marinade and cover well with bread crumb mixture. Place on greased baking pan. Bake at 350° uncovered for 1 hour, or until done.

Optional: Mix ½ cup chopped peanuts with bread crumbs, or sprinkle chicken with sliced, blanched almonds before cooking.

Makes 4 servings.

CHICKEN ORLÉANNE

Representative **Charles Bennett**—*Florida*

> 3 large chicken legs
> 3 large chicken thighs
> 2 large chicken breasts
> lime juice
> salt
> freshly ground pepper
> seasoned flour (seasonings of your choice)
> 4 ounces butter
> 1 clove garlic
> parsley
> rosemary
> 1 stalk celery, chopped
> 3 medium carrots, sliced
> 5 small white onions
> ½ cup dry white wine
> 15½ ounces cream of mushroom soup
> paprika

Brush the chicken pieces with lime juice, season with salt and pepper, and shake in a bag of seasoned flour. Sauté the chicken pieces in a heavy skillet in the butter until they are a golden brown, about 20 minutes. Place a layer of chicken pieces in a casserole dish and sprinkle the layer with ½ clove garlic, minced, a generous pinch of parsley, and a light sprinkling of rosemary. Then add a second layer of chicken pieces and repeat the seasonings on that layer. Sprinkle over the chicken the chopped celery, and place carrots and onions over and around the top.

In the skillet in which the chicken was sautéed, pour the wine and blend it well with the butter remaining in the skillet. Then add the cream of mushroom soup, and again blend the contents of the skillet. Pour this sauce over the casserole and sprinkle the top lightly with pepper and paprika. Bake for 2 hours at 300°.

Makes 8 servings.

CHICKEN CACCIATORE II

Representative **Lee Hamilton**—*Indiana*

 3 pounds fryer chicken, cut in pieces
   olive oil
 1 large onion, sliced
 2 cloves garlic
 8 ounces tomato sauce
20 ounces Italian plum tomatoes
   pepper to taste
 1 teaspoon crushed basil
 1 bay leaf
 ¼ cup white wine

Brown skinned fryer pieces in a bit of olive oil. Remove from pan. Sauté onion cut in ¼-inch slices and garlic in pan. Return chicken to skillet. Combine tomato sauce, plum tomatoes, pepper, basil, and bay leaf. Pour over chicken, cover, and simmer for 30 minutes. Stir in white wine and cook uncovered 15 minutes more. Serve with spaghetti and freshly grated Parmesan cheese.

Makes 6 servings.

CHICKEN BREASTS IN PAPRIKA-CREAM SAUCE

Senator **Harry Reid**—*Nevada*

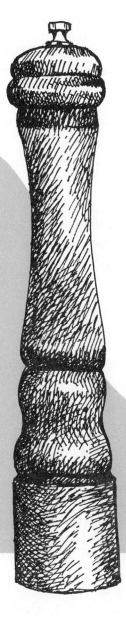

½ cup onions, finely chopped
½ pound butter
1 tablespoon paprika
4 chicken breasts, boned
¼ cup white wine
¼ cup chicken stock
1 cup heavy cream
 salt
 pepper
 lemon juice

Boil onions 3 to 4 minutes. Drain well. Melt butter in casserole dish over low heat. Then add onions, but do not brown onions. Add paprika and remove from heat. Roll chicken breasts in mixture and bake covered at 350° until chicken breasts are done. Remove from oven and set aside.

Reheat sauce mixture and add wine and chicken stock. Bring to a boil and let cook for 3 to 4 minutes. Remove from heat. Add cream and stir well. Cook over low heat for 2 to 3 minutes. Add salt, pepper, and lemon juice to taste. Pour this mixture over baked chicken breasts. Serve with garnish.

Makes 4 servings.

BREAST OF CHICKEN WITH DIJON SAUCE

Senator **Frank Lautenberg**—*New Jersey*

1 cup chicken stock
¼ cup heavy cream
   lemon juice
   salt
   freshly ground black pepper
4 tablespoons Dijon mustard
5 tablespoons lightly salted butter, divided
3 tablespoons finely chopped mixed herbs
   (thyme, parsley, chervil, chives)
2 egg yolks
2 whole chicken breasts, split and skin
   removed
   all purpose flour
   fresh bread crumbs
4 tablespoons clarified butter

Place chicken stock in a small saucepan. Cook until reduced by half. Stir in cream, a dash of lemon juice, salt and pepper to taste, mustard, 4 tablespoons of the butter, and herbs. Stir 2 tablespoons of the sauce into the egg yolks, then add yolks to sauce mixture. Stir over low heat until thickened. Set sauce aside.

Dip chicken in flour to coat lightly. Shake off excess. Brush on small amount of the sauce mixture, then coat very well with bread crumbs.

Heat clarified butter in a 10-inch skillet. When hot, add remaining tablespoon lightly salted butter and coated chicken. Cook for 10 minutes or until nicely browned. Turn, cook 10 minutes.

Let rest for 5 minutes before slicing. Cut each piece on the diagonal into four slices. Place sauce on 4 serving plates. Fan chicken slices over sauce on one side of plate.

Makes 4 servings.

SWEET SOUR CHICKEN

Senator **Spark Matsunaga**—*Hawaii*

2 **pounds chicken wings**
   garlic salt
1 **cup cornstarch**
2 **eggs, well beaten**
4 **tablespoons catsup**
¾ **cup sugar**
½ **cup vinegar**
1 **tablespoon soy sauce**

Cut wings into 3 sections at joints. Discard wing tips. Season wings with garlic salt. Coat wings with cornstarch and dip in eggs before frying in hot oil. Drain.

Combine catsup, sugar, vinegar, and soy sauce and bring to a boil. Place wings in flat pan and pour sauce over wings. Bake at 300° for 30 minutes.

Makes 10 servings.

FAVORITE CHICKEN

Senator **Mark O. Hatfield**—*Oregon*

½ pound dried chipped ham
8 slices bacon
4 whole chicken breasts, boned and halved
10½ ounces cream of mushroom soup
1 teaspoon curry powder
1 pint sour cream, or ½ cup cooking sherry

Tear chipped ham in small bits and scatter in bottom of casserole. Wrap a slice of bacon around each piece of chicken and secure with toothpick. Place on chipped ham. Mix together soup, curry powder, and sour cream (or sherry). Pour mixture over chicken. Bake uncovered at 300° for 3 hours.

Makes 4 to 6 servings.

CHICKEN ROULADES

Senator **James Exon**—*Nebraska*

> ¼ **cup margarine**
> ¼ **cup all-purpose flour**
> ½ **teaspoon salt**
> 1 **teaspoon instant chicken bouillon**
> ½ **cup button mushrooms and liquid**
>   **milk**
> ¼ **cup sherry**
> 8 **slices of Swiss cheese**
> 8 **thin slices cooked ham**
> 4 **whole chicken breasts, boned and halved**

In medium saucepan, melt margarine over low heat. Blend in flour, salt, and bouillon. Drain mushroom liquid into measuring cup. Add milk to make 2 cups. Gradually stir mushroom liquid and milk into flour mixture. Place over medium heat and stir until sauce thickens. Add sherry and mushrooms. Roll 1 slice of cheese and 1 slice of ham together (roll tightly) and wrap chicken breasts around each roll. Place rolled chicken breasts seam-side down in greased baking dish. Pour sauce over. Bake at 350° for 45 minutes.

Makes 8 servings.

CHICKEN-BROCCOLI DIVAN

Representative **William Clinger**—*Pennsylvania*

> 4 **tablespoons butter**
> 3 **tablespoons flour**
> 1 **tablespoon curry powder**
> ½ **teaspoon salt**
> ¼ **teaspoon pepper**
> 1 **cup chicken broth**
> 1 **cup milk**
> 2 **cups cooked chicken, diced**
> 21 **ounces frozen chopped broccoli, thawed
>   and drained**
> ½ **cup shredded cheddar cheese**
> ¼ **cup seasoned, dry bread crumbs**

In saucepan, melt butter and stir in flour, curry powder, salt, and pepper. Gradually stir in chicken broth and milk. Bring mixture to a boil, stirring constantly. Stir in chicken. Remove from heat. Sprinkle broccoli into greased 9 x 13-inch baking dish. Pour chicken mixture over broccoli.

Stir together cheese and crumbs. Sprinkle over casserole. Bake at 400° for 25 to 30 minutes, or until heated through and bubbly.

Makes 6 to 8 servings.

CHICKEN SCALLOPINI

Senator **Alfonse D'Amato**—*New York*

> 3 tablespoons butter
> ½ cup corn oil
> 6 chicken cutlets
> ½ clove garlic, finely chopped
> ¼ teaspoon rosemary
> ¼ teaspoon oregano
> ¼ cup fresh lemon juice
>   salt and pepper
> 6 ounces sliced mushrooms
> ¼ cup fresh parsley, chopped

Heat butter and oil in heavy skillet over medium flame. When hot, add chicken cutlets. When cutlets are brown, add finely chopped garlic, rosemary, oregano, lemon juice, and salt and pepper to taste. Cover immediately. Let simmer for 2 to 3 minutes. Add mushrooms. Cover again and let cook for 10 to 15 minutes. Before serving, add chopped fresh parsley.

Makes 3 servings.

MEXICANA CHICKEN

Senator **Christopher Bond**—*Missouri*

A festive choice for a simple family meal when teamed with side dishes of salsa, guacamole, chopped lettuce, and sour cream. Originally sampled at a Cape Girardeau patio supper, this buffet dish is great for informal entertaining.

10¾ ounces cream of chicken soup
10½ ounces cream of celery soup
10½ ounces chicken broth
4 ounces green chilies
12 corn tortillas, broken into small pieces
3 cups cooked chicken, chopped
8 ounces cheddar cheese, grated

Combine soups, broth, chilies, and tortillas. Let stand 30 minutes. Preheat oven to 350°. Place ½ of the mixture in a greased 9 x 13-inch baking dish. Cover with chicken. Pour remaining mixture over chicken and sprinkle with cheese. Bake uncovered for 25 minutes.

Makes 8 to 10 servings.

LEMON CHICKEN

President **George Bush**

> 6 **boneless chicken breasts**
> 1 **lemon, halved**
> **salt and pepper**
> **flour**
> 2 **tablespoons butter**
> 2 **tablespoons vermouth**
> 1 **cup heavy cream**
> 2 **tablespoons lemon juice**
> **grated rind of 1 lemon**
> **Parmesan cheese**

Rub chicken breasts with lemon, salt, pepper, and a little flour. Sauté in butter 7 minutes on each side. Remove from heat and arrange in a baking dish. Add vermouth, cream, lemon juice, and grated lemon rind to sauté pan. Heat thoroughly, scraping the pan to deglaze it. Strain sauce and pour over chicken breasts. Sprinkle Parmesan cheese over top and brown lightly under broiler a few minutes.

Makes 6 servings.

SMOKED ROASTING HEN

Representative **Clay Shaw**—*Florida*

>   **6- or 7-pound roasting hen**
> **²/₃ cup olive oil**
> **¹/₃ cup vinegar**
>   **5 cloves garlic**
> **½ lemon, juiced**
>   **Worcestershire sauce**
>   **Louisiana Hot Sauce or Durkee's**
>   **Hot Sauce**
>   **pepper**
>   **soy sauce**

Place roasting hen in a pan. Baste with sauce mixture of all other ingredients. Add sauces according to your taste. Place pan in a smoker and smoke for 1½ hours.

Makes 12 to 14 servings.

ROAST DUCK

Representative **Beverly Byron**—*Maryland*

4- **to 5-pound oven-ready duck**
  salt
  pepper
1 **small onion, sliced**
2 **bay leaves**

Wash the duck and pat dry. Season inside with remaining ingredients. Roast at 400° for 30 minutes per pound. Baste with pan juices and drain off excess fat as it accumulates. Serve hot or cold.

Makes 10 servings.

CRAB IMPERIAL

Senator **Spark Matsunaga**—*Hawaii*

Hawaii is blessed with an abundance and variety of foods. It is also a paradise for gourmets, where food from all over the world is served and enjoyed by islanders and visitors alike. In this respect, homemakers in Hawaii are very fortunate. They can have an adventure in cooking while providing for the health and well-being of their families. Good cooking can contribute immeasurably to the happiness of a home.

¼ **cup margarine**
2 **tablespoons flour**
1 **cup milk**
   salt, pepper, and cayenne pepper
1 **egg, slightly beaten**
   dash of dry mustard
1 **teaspoon mayonnaise**
   chopped parsley
1 **pound backfin crabmeat**
   bread crumbs

In a double boiler, make white sauce with margarine, flour, and milk. Add salt, pepper, and cayenne. Remove from heat. Add egg gradually to mixture, followed by mustard, mayonnaise, and parsley. Add crabmeat to mixture. Pour into casserole dish. Top with bread crumbs and dot with butter. Bake at 375° for 15 minutes, or until golden brown.

Makes 4 to 6 servings.

COCO'S SHRIMP AND RICE

Representative **Porter Goss**—*Florida*

It is very rich and great for company!

¼ **pound (or less) butter, melted**
1 **pint cream**
4 **tablespoons Worcestershire sauce**
½ **teaspoon Tabasco**
6 **tablespoons catsup**
2 **cups cooked rice**
2 **cups cooked shrimp**

Combine all ingredients and bake at 350° for approximately 1 hour.

Makes 4 to 6 servings.

IMPERIAL CRAB

Senator **Barbara Mikulski**—*Maryland*

>1 **pound backfin crabmeat**
>**salt**
>**cayenne (red pepper)**
>1 **green pepper, diced**
>2 **eggs, well beaten (save out 2 tablespoons)**
>5 **tablespoons mayonnaise, divided**
>1 **tablespoon onion, chopped**

Pick over crabmeat. Combine with salt, dash of red pepper, green pepper, beaten eggs, mayonnaise, and chopped onion. Fill 6 decorative serving shells with crabmeat mixture. Add 1 tablespoon mayonnaise to remaining egg and put over each filled shell. Dot with red pepper. Bake at 350° for about 30 minutes.

Makes 6 servings.

NORFOLK CRAB CAKES

Senator **John Warner**—*Virginia*

*This is a creative recipe and the
precise measurements,
preparation of the mix and
cooking variables are trade
secrets known only to the chef!
Traditional crab cakes are those
made with a mix of the
ingredients recommended above
and the amounts to suit the
chef's particular taste.*

**fresh onions, preferably two types for a
variety of flavor and texture**
green bell peppers
fresh Chesapeake Bay blue crabmeat
eggs
bread crumbs
pepper
vegetable salt
heavy cream
butter
parsley

Precook onions, taking care not to lose firmness of
texture. Lightly sauté green bell peppers to release
full flavor. Mix crab, onions, green peppers, eggs,
bread crumbs, pepper, and small amount of salt
(crabmeat is naturally slightly salty). Add a touch of
cream.

Sauté butter until brown and quickly add parsley to
release parsley's natural flavor. Form cakes and drop
in butter, cooking sparingly as not to lose the
enhanced fresh crab flavor. Remove and serve.

FLOUNDER FLORENTINE

Representative **Douglas Applegate**—*Ohio*

1½ **pounds flounder or cod**
1 **package frozen spinach soufflé, thawed**
   paprika
   salt and pepper
   lemon juice

Preheat over to 350°. Rinse and dry the flounder.
Cut each flounder filet in half, lengthwise. Spread a
generous amount of spinach soufflé on the fish. Roll
the fish loosely and secure with a toothpick. Place in
baking dish. Spoon the remainder of the spinach in
between the rolls of flounder. Sprinkle with paprika,
salt, and pepper. Cover and bake for 40 minutes.
Remove cover and bake an additional 5 minutes.
Sprinkle with lemon juice and serve.

Makes 4 servings.

SUPER FISH

Senator **Chuck Grassley**—*Iowa*

This is another of my mother's creations. She cooks it in the microwave these days!

3 pounds frozen haddock or cod filets
salt to taste
1 cup sour cream
1 can cream of mushroom soup
1 can cream of celery soup
2 to 3 tablespoons onion, sautéed in butter
parsley

Thaw fish and place in 8 x 12 Pyrex baking dish, still in block size. Sprinkle with salt. Mix all other ingredients except parsley and heat together. Pour over fish and bake for 30 to 40 minutes at 375°, or until fish is done. Sprinkle with parsley before baking or put fresh parsley on top a few minutes before finished baking.

Makes 6 to 8 servings.

FILET OF SOLE

Representative **Richard Gephardt**—*Missouri*

chopped green onions
3 pounds sole or flounder
salt and pepper to taste
¾ cup white wine
1½ cups water
4 tablespoons butter
4 tablespoons flour
¾ cup milk
2 egg yolks
¼ cup cream
lemon juice
¾ pound shrimp
3 tablespoons grated Swiss cheese

Preheat oven to 350°. Butter bottom of shallow baking dish. Sprinkle with chopped green onions. Lay filets over them. Season with salt and pepper. Pour in white wine and water to come almost to top of fish. Bring to slow simmer on stove. Cover dish and bake in oven for 10 minutes. Drain off liquid and save for sauce.

In a 2-quart pan, melt the butter. Stir in flour slowly, and continue stirring over flame for 1 to 2 minutes. Remove from heat and add poaching liquid and milk. Return to high heat and stir until it thickens and comes to a boil. Let simmer for 1 minute. Mix egg yolks with the cream. Stir in 2 tablespoons of hot mixture and then 2 more. Add egg and cream mixture to hot sauce and bring to a boil over moderate heat. Boil for 30 seconds. Remove from heat. Add 1 or 2 drops of lemon juice, and salt and pepper to taste. Sauce should lightly coat spoon. If more liquid has accumulated in baking dish add to sauce.

Cover sole with shrimp and then sauce and Swiss cheese. Bake in top third of oven for 10 to 15 minutes, or until sauce bubbles, at 425°.

Makes 6 servings.

SAUTÉED TROUT
WITH FRESH TARRAGON

Senator **Daniel P. Moynihan**—*New York*

> 2 **small brook trout, gutted and washed and
>   dried with paper towels**
> 4 **tablespoons butter**
>   **fresh tarragon leaves, roughly cut,
>   generous handful**
>   **salt**
>   **pepper**
>   **juice of 1 lemon**

In a frying pan large enough to hold both fish, melt butter until nut brown in color, carefully watching so that it does not burn. Add fish, tarragon, seasonings, and lemon juice and cook on one side for about 3½ minutes. Turn trout gently with two wooden spatulas and continue to cook for about 4 to 5 minutes, or until springy when touched and fork shows flesh is flaky.

Remove fish from pan and insert a sharp knife at the back of the trout's head, run knife along the back and underside and the whole bone will be exposed. Lift tail and it will come off intact with the head. Place filets on plates and divide sauce from pan.

Makes 2 servings.

TROUT AND GINGER

Senator **Malcolm Wallop**—*Wyoming*

>   1 egg
> ⅓ cup milk
> ⅓ cup water
> ½ cup corn meal
> ½ cup cake flour
>   salt and pepper to taste
>   6 fresh trout
>   2 tablespoons fresh grated ginger
>   bacon grease or vegetable shortening

Beat egg and combine with milk and water. Mix together corn meal, cake flour, salt, and pepper. Dip trout in egg-and-milk mixture, and then roll it in flour mixture. Sprinkle ginger in open cavities. Sauté in bacon grease or shortening over medium-hot flame until done.

Makes 6 generous servings.

BAKED SHAD AND ROE

Senator **William Roth**—*Delaware*

1 medium to large shad, split
1 set shad roe
½ pint sour cream
paprika
lemon slices

Place fish in shallow baking dish, skin side down. Lay piece of roe on each piece of fish. Cover fish and roe with thick layer of sour cream. Sprinkle with paprika. Put lemon slices on each piece of fish. Bake for 30 minutes at 400°.

Makes 4 servings.

BROILED SWORDFISH

Senator **John H. Chafee**—*Rhode Island*

> 4 pounds skinless, boneless swordfish
> 1 medium onion, chopped
>   pinch of dried thyme
>   pinch of dried tarragon
> 1 bay leaf
> 1 lemon, juiced
>   corn oil
> 4 medium green peppers
> 1 pound fresh button mushrooms
>   butter
>   lemon juice
>   salt and pepper to taste

Cut swordfish into cubes, approximately 2 ounces each (4 cubes per person). Place cubes in a bowl and add onion, thyme, tarragon, bay leaf, and lemon juice. Cover with corn oil and marinate in refrigerator overnight.

Cut green pepper into quarters and remove seeds. Boil green pepper quarters for 5 minutes. Drain. Sauté mushroom caps in butter with a drop of lemon juice for 5 minutes. Remove swordfish cubes from oil and place on skewers, alternating with mushrooms and green peppers. Sprinkle with salt and pepper and broil for 15 minutes turning frequently. Serve on rice.

Makes 6 to 8 servings.

Breads

Yeast Breads

Quick Breads

Muffins

Pancakes

Waffles

SIX-GRAIN BREAD

Senator **Lloyd Bentsen**—*Texas*

This multi-grained, country bread recipe is a family favorite that has been enjoyed by several generations of Bentsens. I prefer it to cake!

1 cup milk
½ tablespoon vegetable oil
1 teaspoon salt
⅓ cup maple syrup or honey
1 tablespoon blackstrap molasses
1 tablespoon dry yeast
¼ cup warm water
½ teaspoon sugar or honey
2 cups unbleached white flour
¼ cup raw sunflower kernels
⅛ cup wheat germ
⅛ cup Miller's bran
¼ cup rye flour
1½ cups whole-wheat flour

Scald the milk in a medium saucepan. Add oil, salt, maple syrup, and molasses, stirring to mix. Cool mixture at room temperature.

In a large mixing bowl, dissolve yeast in the warm water with ½ teaspoon of sugar or honey. When the mixture appears frothy, add the scalded milk along with white flour. Beat for 2 minutes with an electric mixer, or 200 strokes by hand. Mix in sunflower kernels, wheat germ, bran, and rye flour. Begin to add whole-wheat flour in small amounts until the dough clings together and leaves the sides of the bowl.

Turn the dough out onto a floured surface and knead until the texture is smooth and elastic. Add more whole-wheat flour if the dough is sticky. Put dough in buttered bowl, turning it around to coat all sides. Cover bowl with a damp cloth and let it rise until doubled in bulk. Punch the dough down. Turn it onto a floured surface, knead to press out air bubbles, cut into 3 equal parts, and cover with the cloth. Let the dough rest for 10 minutes.

Shape the pieces into loaves and place in 3 medium-sized, greased loaf pans. Brush the tops with melted butter. Cover with the cloth and let rise again until almost doubled. Preheat oven to 350°. Bake for 35 minutes, or until the bottoms sound hollow when tapped. Remove loaves from the pans and cool on racks.

Makes 3 loaves.

SOUTHWEST VIRGINIA BROWN BREAD

Representative **Rick Boucher**—*Virginia*

Southwest Virginia Brown Bread is a traditional favorite in the Fightin' Ninth Congressional District of Virginia.

1 cup brown sugar
1 cup dark molasses
3 packages dry yeast
2 tablespoons salt
2 cups dry milk
7 cups very warm water
5 tablespoons melted shortening
3 eggs, lightly beaten
9 cups whole-wheat flour
8 to 9 cups all-purpose flour

Mix all ingredients except all-purpose flour and let stand 15 minutes. Add enough all-purpose flour to make slightly sticky but elastic dough (8 to 9 cups). Knead thoroughly for about 7 minutes.

Cover dough with clean cloth and let rise in warm, draft-free place until it doubles in bulk. Punch down and let rise again until it doubles in bulk. Shape into loaves and let rise in greased bread pans until more than double. Bake at 350° until done, about 45 minutes.

Makes 7 loaves.

MARY'S SPOON BREAD

Representative **Jim Bunning**—*Kentucky*

> 1 cup corn meal
> 2 cups milk, scalded
> ½ teaspoon salt
> 1 tablespoon sugar
> 1 cup margarine
> 5 eggs, separated
> 1½ tablespoons bourbon

Add corn meal to scalded milk. Continue cooking and stirring until thick. Add salt, sugar, and margarine and heat until margarine is melted. Add beaten egg yolks to mixture. Fold in egg whites (beaten until stiff) and add bourbon. Bake in a 2-quart, greased casserole for 40 minutes at 350°. Serve immediately.

Makes 6 to 8 servings.

WHOLE-MEAL IRISH SODA BREAD

Representative **Porter Goss**—*Florida*

Makes wonderful toast!

½ cup white flour, sifted
1½ cups whole-wheat flour
½ teaspoon salt
1 tablespoon sugar
1 teaspoon baking soda
½ teaspoon cream of tartar
2 tablespoons shortening
¾ cup buttermilk

Mix dry ingredients with a fork. Add shortening and buttermilk. If too dry, add more buttermilk. Knead 10 times. Form a circular loaf. Cut a deep 1-inch cross in the top. Bake on a cookie sheet for 50 minutes at 375°.

CORN BREAD

Senator **Spark Matsunaga**—*Hawaii*

> 2 cups Bisquick
> ½ cup sugar
> ½ teaspoon baking soda
> 1 teaspoon baking powder
> ½ cup corn meal
> 2 eggs
> 1 cup milk
> 1 cup butter or margarine, melted

Measure dry ingredients. Beat eggs, add milk and butter. Mix with dry ingredients. Bake at 350° for 35 to 40 minutes in 9-inch square pan.

MILK BISCUITS

Representative **Beverly Byron**—*Maryland*

> 2 **cups flour**
> ½ **teaspoon salt**
> 1 **tablespoon plus 1 teaspoon baking powder**
> ½ **teaspoon cream of tartar**
> 2 **tablespoons sugar**
> 8 **tablespoons solid shortening**
> ⅔ **cup milk**

Combine first 5 ingredients in a mixing bowl. Add shortening and cut in with two knives. Pour milk over ingredients and stir quickly into dough. Knead lightly 5 times, and roll out on floured board to ½ inch thick. Cut into 2-inch rounds. Bake at 450° on a lightly greased cookie sheet for 10 to 12 minutes.

GEORGIA PEACH BREAD

Senator **Sam Nunn**—*Georgia*

3 cups fresh peaches, sliced
6 tablespoons sugar
2 cups all-purpose flour
1 teaspoon baking soda
¼ teaspoon salt
1 teaspoon ground cinnamon
1½ cups sugar
½ cup shortening
2 eggs
1 cup pecans, finely chopped
1 teaspoon vanilla

Place peaches and 6 tablespoons of sugar in blender and process until pureed. Mixture should yield about 2¼ cups. Combine flour, baking soda, salt, and cinnamon and set aside.

Cream 1½ cups sugar and shortening. Add eggs and mix well. Add peach puree and dry ingredients until moistened. Stir in nuts and vanilla. Spoon batter into 2 well-greased and floured 9 x 5 x 3-inch loaf pans. Bake at 325° for 55 to 60 minutes, or until done. Cool 10 minutes in pan and then turn on rack and cool completely.

Makes 2 loaves.

POPPY SEED BREAD OR CAKE

Representative **Dan Schaefer**—*Colorado*

> 4 eggs
> 2 cups sugar
> 1½ cups oil
> 3 cups flour
> 1½ teaspoons baking soda
> 1½ teaspoons salt
> 13 ounces evaporated milk
> 2 ounces poppy seeds

In a large mixing bowl, beat eggs well. Add sugar slowly, beating in well. Add the oil slowly and beat well. Sift together flour, soda, and salt and add slowly to mixture. Beat thoroughly.

Add evaporated milk and beat well. Add poppy seeds and beat well. Bake in an ungreased angel food pan, or greased and floured Bundt pan, for 1¼ hours at 350°. Remove from pan after cooling for 10 minutes. For angel food pan, turn upside down until cool.

PUMPKIN BREAD

Senator **Spark Matsunaga**—*Hawaii*

3½ cups flour, sifted
2 teaspoons baking soda
1 teaspoon salt
3 teaspoons cinnamon
1 teaspoon nutmeg
3 cups sugar
4 eggs, slightly beaten
1 cup salad oil
⅔ cup water
2 cups pumpkin, canned
1 cup chopped nuts
1 cup raisins

Mix all ingredients well and bake in loaf pans at 325° for 90 minutes.

Makes 3 loaves.

ALMOND BREAD

Representative **Fred Grandy**—*Iowa*

> 1 cup Grapenuts cereal
> 3 cups cold milk
> 1 tablespoon butter
> 2 eggs
> 1½ cups sugar
> ½ pound almond paste
> 3 cups flour
> 2 tablespoons baking powder
> 1 tablespoon baking soda

Set Grapenuts cereal and cold milk, mixed, in a bowl in refrigerator overnight. Beat the butter, eggs, and sugar until creamy. Cream the almond paste into the egg mixture. Sift together the flour, baking powder, and baking soda. Add this to the egg mixture alternately with the milk mixture. Bake at 350° for 1 hour in heavily greased and floured pans. Freezes well!

Makes 2 loaves.

BANANA BREAD I

Representative **Gerry Sikorski**—*Minnesota*

*This is my favorite recipe from
Grandma Nettie.*

½ **cup butter**
¾ **cup sugar**
2 **eggs**
3 **bananas**
2 **cups flour**
¼ **teaspoon salt**
1 **teaspoon baking soda**
4 **tablespoons sour milk**

Cream butter. Add sugar gradually. Add beaten
eggs. Add mashed bananas, then sifted flour and
salt. Add baking soda alternately with sour milk.
Bake for 30 minutes in a loaf pan at 350°.

Makes 1 loaf.

BANANA BREAD II

Senator **Daniel Inouye**—*Hawaii*

>   2 **cups enriched flour, sifted**
>   2 **teaspoons baking powder**
> ¾ **teaspoon salt**
> ½ **teaspoon baking soda**
>   1 **cup Hawaiian cane sugar**
>   2 **eggs**
>   1 **cup mashed bananas**
> ½ **cup shortening**
>   1 **teaspoon lemon juice**
>   1 **cup macadamia nuts, chopped**

Sift together flour, baking powder, salt, baking soda, and sugar into bowl. Add eggs and ½ cup bananas to shortening. Stir to combine ingredients, then beat 2 minutes at medium speed on electric mixer, or 300 strokes by hand. Add remaining bananas and lemon juice. Beat 2 minutes more. Fold in ¾ cup nuts.

Pour into greased, lined loaf pan 8½ x 4½ inches. Sprinkle ¼ cup nuts over top of batter. Bake in a moderate 350° oven for 1 hour.

Makes 1 loaf.

NO-BEAT POPOVERS

Senator **Spark Matsunaga**—*Hawaii*

    2 eggs
    1 cup milk
    1 cup flour, sifted
    ½ teaspoon salt

Break eggs into bowl. Add milk, flour, and salt. Mix well with spoon, disregarding lumps. Fill well-greased muffin pan ¾ full. Put into cold oven. Set controls at 450°. Turn on heat and bake for 25 minutes. The secret: starting with the cold oven—and not peeking for the full 25 minutes. Turn off heat. Slit centers to let air out and leave in oven until the sides brown.

ZUCCHINI MUFFINS

Representative **Ron Packard**—*California*

1½ cups flour
½ teaspoon baking powder
½ teaspoon baking soda
½ teaspoon salt
½ teaspoon nutmeg
2 eggs
1 cup sugar
½ cup cooking oil
2 cups shredded zucchini
½ cup raisins
½ cup chopped nuts

Sift together first five ingredients and set aside. Beat eggs. Add sugar and oil. Gradually add dry ingredients. Stir in zucchini, raisins, and nuts. Fill muffin tins, lined with paper, ⅔ full. Bake at 350° for 25 minutes.

Makes 1 dozen.

PEACH MUFFINS

Senator **Christopher Bond**—*Missouri*

Peaches are an important summer crop in Missouri and nowhere are they more succulent than in the Boot heel. A Kennett luncheon featured this regional specialty.

2 cups unsifted flour
1 tablespoon baking powder
1 egg
¼ cup oil
1 cup milk
⅔ cup sugar
½ teaspoon salt
¼ teaspoon cinnamon
1 teaspoon lemon juice
¼ teaspoon vanilla
1 cup fresh peaches, chopped

Preheat oven to 450°. Sift flour and baking powder together. Beat egg and stir in oil, milk, sugar, salt, cinnamon, lemon juice, and vanilla. Add flour mixture and stir until blended. Do not over-mix. Gently fold in peaches. Fill greased muffin cups ⅔ full. Bake 20 minutes.

Note: A drained 16-ounce can of peaches packed in light syrup or water may be substituted.

Makes 18 to 20 muffins.

BLUEBERRY MUFFINS I

Senator **Tom Daschle**—*South Dakota*

>   1 egg
>   1 cup milk
>   ¼ cup vegetable oil or butter
>   2 cups flour
>   ¼ cup sugar
>   3 teaspoons baking powder
>   1 teaspoon salt
>   1 cup blueberries

Beat egg well, then add milk and oil or butter. Mix the dry ingredients in separate bowl and add liquids. Fold gently. Add the blueberries and fill greased muffin cups ⅔ full. Bake for 15 minutes at 400°.

APPLE MUFFINS

Representative **Gerry Sikorski**—*Minnesota*

½ cup sugar
¼ cup shortening
1 teaspoon salt
1 egg
1 cup milk
1½ cups flour
¼ teaspoon cinnamon
3 teaspoons baking powder
1½ cups apples, chopped and peeled
½ cup flour, sifted
¼ cup brown sugar, firmly packed
¼ teaspoon cinnamon

Combine sugar, shortening, and salt. Add egg and beat well. Stir in milk. Sift together flour, cinnamon, and baking powder. Stir flour into other mixture and blend just until flour is moist. Add chopped apples which have been coated with ½ cup flour. Blend carefully. Divide batter into 12 well-greased muffin tins. Sprinkle with combined brown sugar and cinnamon. Bake at 400° for 20 to 25 minutes. Serve warm.

BLUEBERRY MUFFINS II

Senator **Warren Rudman**—*New Hampshire*

  1 **cup sugar**
  ½ **cup butter**
  1 **teaspoon vanilla**
  2 **eggs**
  2 **cups unsifted flour**
  2 **teaspoons baking powder**
  ½ **teaspoon salt**
  ½ **cup milk**
2½ **cups blueberries**
  2 **teaspoons sugar for topping**

Cream sugar, butter, and vanilla until frothy. Add eggs one at a time and beat. Sift dry ingredients. Add alternately with milk. Mash half the blueberries and stir into above by hand. Add remaining, whole blueberries by hand. Do not beat.

Grease muffin pan top and interior, or use paper muffin holders. Pile mixture high in each cup. Sprinkle sugar on top. Bake at 350° for 30 minutes. Cool at least 30 minutes.

OATMEAL PANCAKES

Senator **Chuck Grassley**—*Iowa*

From Mary, my neighbor in Virginia.

2 eggs, beaten
1½ cups buttermilk
1 cup oatmeal
1 teaspoon baking powder
1 teaspoon baking soda
½ teaspoon salt
1 teaspoon sugar
⅓ cup flour

Mix and let set a few minutes for oatmeal to soak up a bit of moisture. Cook in a hot skillet as you do other pancakes.

Makes 8 pancakes.

IDAHO APPLE WAFFLES

Senator **Steve Symms**—*Idaho*

>   2 **cups milk**
>   2 **eggs**
>   2 **cups pancake mix**
>   ⅓ **cup butter or margarine, melted**
>   1 **cup Idaho Jonathan or Rome apples,**
>   **finely chopped**

Place milk, eggs, pancake mix, and melted butter in a bowl. Beat with rotary beater until batter is fairly smooth. Stir in apples. Bake in a hot waffle baker until steaming stops. Serve with butter and cinnamon sugar.

Makes 6 servings.

Cakes and Cookies

GOOEY BUTTER
COFFEE CAKE

Senator **Christopher Bond**—*Missouri*

Long a St. Louis favorite. We discovered the "goodie" at a campaign coffee in Florissant.

  1 **16-ounce box pound cake mix**
  4 **eggs**
 ½ **cup butter, melted**
16 **ounces confectioners' sugar**
  8 **ounces cream cheese, softened**
1½ **teaspoons vanilla extract**

Preheat oven to 350°. Combine cake mix, 2 of the eggs, and butter. Pour into a well-greased 9 x 13-inch baking pan. Reserve 2 tablespoons of sugar. Combine cream cheese, vanilla, remaining eggs, and sugar. Mix well and spread over batter. Bake for 15 minutes. Remove from oven, sprinkle reserved sugar on top. Return to oven, continue to bake for 25 minutes. Cool on rack or serve warm.

Makes 10 to 12 servings.

APPLE CAKE

Representative **Ron Packard**—*California*

2 tablespoons margarine
2 cups sugar
3 medium eggs
2 teaspoons baking soda
1 teaspoon cinnamon
1 teaspoon nutmeg
½ teaspoon salt
2 cups flour
½ cup nuts, chopped
5 apples, chopped

Cream margarine and sugar, add eggs. Sift dry ingredients and add gradually to mixture. Add apples and nuts last. Grease and flour large rectangular cake pan. Bake at 375° for 45 minutes, or test with toothpick.

APPLE DAPPLE CAKE

Senator **Christopher Bond**—*Missouri*

No trip to Pike County is complete without a visit to the Stark Apple Orchards in Louisiana. Governor and Mrs. Lloyd Stark were longtime family friends. During the restoration of the Governor's Mansion, Mrs. Stark could not have been more helpful or supportive.

3 **eggs**
1½ **cups salad oil**
2 **cups sugar**
3 **cups flour**
1 **teaspoon salt**
1 **teaspoon baking soda**
4 **cups apples, chopped**
1½ **cups pecans, chopped**
2 **teaspoons vanilla**
Glaze:
1 **cup brown sugar**
¼ **cup milk**
½ **cup margarine**

Preheat oven to 350°. Mix eggs, oil, and sugar and blend well. Sift flour, salt, and baking soda together and add to egg mixture. Add apples, nuts, and vanilla. Pour batter into greased tube or Bundt pan. Bake for 1 hour.

Remove from oven. In saucepan, combine brown sugar, milk, and margarine. Simmer 2½ minutes. While cake is still hot, pour glaze over cake in pan. Cool cake completely before removing from pan.

Makes 18 servings.

CHOCOLATE CHOCOLATE ANGEL FOOD CAKE

Senator **John Rockefeller**—*West Virginia*

    12 large egg whites
     1 teaspoon cream of tartar
  1¼ cups superfine sugar
     ¼ teaspoon salt
     1 teaspoon vanilla
     ¾ cup cake flour
     ¼ cup cocoa powder
     ¼ cup chocolate syrup

Preheat oven to 325°. Beat egg whites in a large bowl for a few minutes before adding the cream of tartar. Beat until the egg whites stand in stiff peaks. Combine the sugar and salt (if using granulated sugar, sift the sugar twice) and add slowly to the egg whites; also add the vanilla at this point. Continue beating until peaks are stiff and shiny. Sift the flour and cocoa powder together and add to the above, stirring slowly.

Spoon into an ungreased angel food cake tin, preferably with a removable bottom. After filling up half the pan, being careful not to form air bubbles, drizzle chocolate syrup over the top of the mixture and plunge a spatula down into the mixture in about four spots. Add the remaining batter and again add chocolate syrup and repeat the plunge, in different sections this time. Keep in mind that an overdose of chocolate will be too heavy for the batter to support and it will consequently sink through the cake while baking and settle on the bottom, making the cake too heavy and moist.

Place into oven and bake for about 50 to 60 minutes. Remove from oven and stand on the neck of a bottle until completely cool. Run a serrated knife around the inner tube and the outside of the cake pan releasing it. Remove and do the same for the bottom of the pan. Place on a cake platter and serve.

KAHLUA CHOCOLATE FUDGE CAKE

Senator **Joseph Biden**—*Delaware*

Pecan pan coat:
- 1 tablespoon butter
- ¼ cup pecans, finely chopped
- 1 teaspoon sugar

Cake:
- ¾ cup unsweetened cocoa powder
- 1 cup boiling water
- ½ cup Kahlua
- 1⅔ cups sifted all-purpose flour
- 1 teaspoon baking soda
- ½ teaspoon baking powder
- ½ teaspoon salt
- ¾ cup butter
- 1½ cups sugar
- 3 large eggs, beaten
- 3 tablespoons raspberry jam

Kahlua frosting:
- 6 ounces semisweet chocolate morsels
- ½ cup butter
- 1 teaspoon instant coffee granules
- ¼ cup Kahlua

For pecan pan coat: Butter sides of a 9-inch springform pan. Spread 1 tablespoon butter in bottom of pan. Sprinkle with pecans and 1 teaspoon sugar. Set aside.

For cake: Mix cocoa with boiling water and cool. Add ¼ cup Kahlua. Mix flour, soda, baking powder, and salt together. Put aside. Cream butter and sugar until fluffy and add beaten eggs. Blend dry ingredients into cream mixture alternately with cocoa mixture. Pour into springform pan. Bake at 325° for 60 to 70 minutes. Cool in pan for 10 minutes only. Remove sides and let cool. (Take pan coat side as bottom of cake.) Cut cake in half horizontally, and drizzle remaining Kahlua over each half. Spread jam over bottom layer.

For frosting: Melt chocolate morsels on top of double boiler. Gradually beat in ½ cup butter and instant coffee granules dissolved in a ¼ cup Kahlua. Beat until smooth. Spread ¼ cup of Kahlua frosting over jam. Place top on cake and frost all over. Cake should rest overnight.

CURRENT RIVER CHOCOLATE SHEET CAKE

Senator **Christopher Bond**—*Missouri*

Always tucked away in a cooler for our float trips on the Current River, this delicious, yet easy dessert is the first to disappear at a carry-in supper.

1 cup butter
½ cup cocoa
1 cup water
2 cups sugar
2 cups flour, unsifted
1 teaspoon baking soda
2 eggs, slightly beaten
½ cup sour cream
2 teaspoons vanilla

Chocolate nut icing:
½ cup butter
¼ cup cocoa
6 tablespoons evaporated milk
16 ounces confectioners' sugar
1 cup chopped nuts
1 teaspoon vanilla

Preheat oven to 350°. Thoroughly grease a 15½ x 10½-inch jelly roll pan. Combine butter, cocoa, and water in a saucepan and bring to a full boil. While still hot, pour mixture over combined sugar, flour, and baking soda. Mix well. Add eggs, sour cream, and vanilla. Mix well. Pour batter into pan, bake 15 minutes. Do not overbake.

While cake is baking, make the icing. Mix butter, cocoa, and milk in a saucepan; heat to boiling point. Add confectioners' sugar, nuts, and vanilla and mix well. Additional milk may be added to make icing more spreadable. Ice cake immediately after removing from oven.

Makes 20 to 24 servings.

RHUBARB CAKE

Senator **Chuck Grassley**—*Iowa*

From Esther, who has given my wife many great recipes.

1 cup sugar
1 cup sour cream
1 egg
1½ cups flour
1 teaspoon baking soda
½ teaspoon salt
3 cups freshly cut rhubarb, chopped
1 teaspoon vanilla
1 cup brown sugar
1 teaspoon cinnamon

Using a mixer, beat together the sugar, sour cream, and egg. Add the flour, soda, and salt. Stir in the rhubarb by hand. Pour in a greased 9 x 13-inch pan. Top with mixture of vanilla, brown sugar, and cinnamon. Bake at 375° for 40 to 45 minutes.

COCOA CAKE

Senator **Chuck Grassley**—*Iowa*

This is one of my mother-in-law's favorite standbys. My wife has been making it since she was in high school.

1½ cups sugar
½ cup shortening
½ teaspoon salt
2 eggs
¾ cup sour milk or buttermilk
1 teaspoon soda
1½ cups flour
3 heaping tablespoons cocoa
1 teaspoon vanilla
½ cup boiling water

Cream the sugar, shortening, and salt. Add eggs and beat. Mix buttermilk and soda and add to creamed mixture, alternately with flour and cocoa. Add vanilla. Last, add boiling water. Pour batter into greased 9 x 13-inch pan. Bake for 35 minutes at 350°.

MACADAMIA NUT
ICEBOX CAKE

Senator **Spark Matsunaga**—*Hawaii*

> ¼ cup cold water
> 1 envelope unflavored gelatin
> 4 egg yolks
>   pinch of salt
> ½ cup, plus 2 tablespoons, sugar
> 2 cups milk, scalded
> ½ teaspoon vanilla
> 1½ cups heavy cream
> 3½ ounces macadamia nuts, finely chopped
> 14 whole ladyfingers, split

Soften gelatin in cold water. Set in pan of simmering water and stir until dissolved. Remove from heat but leave in water to stay warm. Beat yolks, adding salt and ¼ cup of the sugar. Gradually stir in milk and cook over low heat, stirring constantly until mixture coats spoon. Add vanilla and gelatin and cool to room temperature, stirring occasionally to prevent setting.

Beat 1 cup of the cream, gradually adding ¼ cup sugar. Add all but 2 tablespoons of chopped nuts to custard mixture. Fold in cream. Line a 10-inch springform pan, sides and bottom, with split lady-fingers. Pour in mixture and chill. Just before serving, whip remaining heavy cream, adding remaining 2 tablespoons sugar. Spread over custard and decorate with reserved nuts.

DEEP SOUTH SYRUP CAKE

Senator **John Breaux**—*Louisiana*

½ **cup vegetable oil**
1½ **cups cane syrup**
1 **egg, well beaten**
2½ **cups flour, sifted**
1 **teaspoon ginger**
½ **teaspoon salt (optional)**
1½ **teaspoons baking soda**
¾ **cup hot water**
½ **cup chopped pecans or raisins**

Grease and flour a 9 x 13-inch pan. Preheat oven to 350°. Combine oil, syrup, and beaten egg and stir until well blended. Mix dry ingredients except baking soda. Mix soda and hot water and stir until dissolved. Alternate adding hot water mixture and syrup mixture to flour mixture, and stir until well blended. Add pecans or raisins at this time and blend. Pour into prepared pan and bake for 45 minutes. Cut into squares and serve with Cool Whip.

BRINGHURST PECAN CAKE

Representative **John Kasich**—*Ohio*

> 1 cup butter, softened
> 2 cups sugar
> 6 eggs
> 4 cups flour
> 1 teaspoon baking powder
> 1 tablespoon grated nutmeg
> 1 teaspoon allspice
> 1 teaspoon mace
> 1 cup bourbon
> 3 cups raisins, soaked overnight in
>   bourbon (use golden and regular)
> 1 pound pecans, halved

Cream butter in large mixing bowl, gradually add sugar, and beat well. Add eggs one at a time, beating after every addition. Combine 3¾ cups flour, baking powder, and spices. Add to creamed mixture alternately with bourbon, beginning and ending with the flour mixture. Mix well.

Dredge raisins and pecans in remaining ¼ cup flour, stir into batter. Spoon batter into a heavily greased 10-inch tube pan papered with wax paper. Bake at 325° for 1 hour and 15 minutes until cake tests done. Cool cake in pan for 15 minutes. Remove cake from pan and let cake cool completely.

TEXAS PECAN CAKE

Representative **John Kasich**—*Ohio*

2 cups butter or margarine
1 cup sugar
1 cup brown sugar
7 eggs
4 cups flour
2 teaspoons baking powder
1 lemon, juiced, including pulp
1 pound pecans
4½ cups bourbon-soaked raisins

Cream butter in a large mixing bowl, gradually adding sugars. Beat until light and fluffy. Add eggs one at a time, beating well after each addition. Combine 3½ cups flour and baking powder. Gradually add to creamed mixture alternately with lemon juice beginning and ending with flour mixture. Beat well after each addition (batter will be thick).

Dredge pecans and raisins in remaining ½ cup flour, stir into batter. Spoon batter into a greased and floured 10-inch tube pan. Bake at 325° for 1 hour and 45 minutes, or until cake tests done. Cool in pan for 15 minutes. Remove and let cool completely before serving.

POUND CAKE

Senator **Robert Byrd**—*West Virginia*

> 2 cups sugar
> 1 cup white vegetable shortening
> 3 cups flour
> ½ teaspoon baking powder
> ½ teaspoon baking soda
> 4 eggs
> 1 teaspoon vanilla or almond flavoring
> 1 cup buttermilk

Cream sugar and shortening. Sift dry ingredients together and add eggs, flavoring, and half the milk. Beat 2 minutes and add remaining milk. Beat 2 more minutes. Bake in two greased, waxed paper-lined 8 x 3-inch loaf pans at 325° for 45 to 50 minutes.

Makes 2 cake loaves.

ITALIAN CREME CAKE

Representative **Mike Synar**—*Oklahoma*

½ cup white vegetable shortening
½ cup butter
2 cups granulated sugar
5 eggs, separated
1 teaspoon vanilla
2 cups flour
1 teaspoon baking soda
½ teaspoon salt
1 cup buttermilk
1 cup pecans, chopped
1 cup coconut flakes

Frosting:
8 ounces cream cheese
½ cup butter
1 teaspoon vanilla
1 pound powdered sugar
1 cup pecans, chopped
1 cup coconut flakes

Cream shortening and ½ cup butter with granulated sugar. Add egg yolks and vanilla. Blend. Sift together flour, baking soda and salt and add alternately with the buttermilk to the creamed mixture. Add pecans and coconut. Fold in egg whites which have been beaten stiff, but not dry. Pour into three 8-inch layer pans which have been greased and floured and bake at 325° for approximately 40 minutes.

For frosting, blend cream cheese, butter, vanilla, and powdered sugar. Add pecans and coconut. Frost cake when cool.

WHIPPED CREAM POUND CAKE

Representative **Trent Lott**—*Mississippi*

3 cups sugar
1 cup butter, softened
6 eggs, room temperature
3 cups cake flour, sifted
½ pint whipping cream, whipped
2 teaspoons vanilla

Cream sugar and butter. Add eggs one at a time and beat well after each one. Add flour and cream alternately. Add vanilla. Pour in greased and floured large tube pan. Place in cold oven and bake at 325° for 1 hour and 15 minutes.

DAISY'S WHITE CAKE

Representative **Porter Goss**—*Florida*

1 cup butter
2 cups white sugar
3 cups flour, sifted
2 teaspoons baking powder
1 cup milk
6 egg whites, beaten

Cream butter and sugar. Add flour, baking powder, and milk. Stir well. Gently fold in the egg whites last. Bake at 350° for 30 minutes in two well-greased 9-inch pans.

Icing:

3 squares Baker's unsweetened chocolate
1 tablespoon butter
small amount of cream
powdered sugar (approximately one pound)

Melt first three ingredients. Beat in sifted powdered sugar until thick. Spread on cake when cool.

OATMEAL LACE COOKIES

President **George Bush**

> ½ **cup flour**
> ¼ **teaspoon baking powder**
> ½ **cup sugar**
> ½ **cup quick-cooking oats**
> 2 **tablespoons white corn syrup**
> ⅓ **cup butter, melted**
> 1 **tablespoon vanilla**

Sift flour, baking powder, and sugar together. Add remaining ingredients, mixing until well blended. Drop slightly heaping ¼ teaspoonfuls about 4 inches apart onto ungreased cookie sheet. Bake in a preheated 375° oven 6 minutes or until lightly browned. Let stand a few seconds before removing from pan.

Makes 4 dozen cookies.

DOUBLE DIP
CHOCOLATE COOKIES

Senator **Christopher Bond**—*Missouri*

Our son Samuel thinks the extra dip of chocolate makes this a stellar afternoon treat with a cold glass of milk.

1 cup brown sugar
1 cup sugar
1 cup margarine
2 eggs
1 teaspoon vanilla
1 teaspoon baking soda
1 teaspoon salt
3 cups flour
30 ounces semisweet chocolate chips
1 cup pecans, chopped

Preheat oven to 375°. Reserve 12 ounces of chocolate chips for dipping.

Cream sugars, margarine, eggs, and vanilla until light. Add baking soda, salt, and flour gradually, mixing until smooth. Add remaining 18 ounces of chocolate chips and the pecans. Using a measuring teaspoon, drop rounded spoonfuls of dough about 3 inches apart on a foil-covered baking sheet, flattening each mound slightly with palm of hand. Bake 8 to 10 minutes or until done. Remove from baking sheet, cool on rack.

Melt reserved chocolate chips. Dip half of each cooled cookie in chocolate. Spread chocolate evenly over cookie half. If chocolate is too thick, remove excess with a knife. Place cookies on waxed paper. Cool in refrigerator until chocolate hardens.

Makes 4 dozen.

ROSE'S CHOCOLATE CHIP COOKIES

Senator **Robert Kerrey**—*Nebraska*

Rose Schwenke was the cook at the Governor's Mansion, while I was the Governor of Nebraska. Rose has been a very good cook for many years. Although she is now retired, she is still cooking.

1 cup butter-flavored shortening
¾ cup white sugar
¾ cup brown sugar, firmly packed
2 eggs
2¼ cups flour
1 teaspoon salt
1 teaspoon baking soda
2 teaspoons vanilla
12 ounces chocolate chips
1 cup nuts, finely chopped

Cream together shortening, white sugar, and brown sugar. Add eggs, beating well. Sift together flour, salt, and baking soda. Add to creamed mixture. Stir in vanilla, chocolate chips, and nuts. Shape into 1-inch balls. Place 2 inches apart on ungreased cookie sheet. Flatten with the bottom of a glass dipped in white sugar.

Bake at 325° for about 10 minutes. The cookies will look like they are not done. Let set on cookie sheet until cool enough to handle. Bake one sheet at a time.

Makes 48 to 50 cookies.

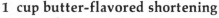

GERMAN CHOCOLATE CARAMEL BARS

Senator **Christopher Bond**—*Missouri*

Grandmother Ida Doerr Bond is believed to be the source for this family favorite from Perryville.

14 ounces caramels
5 ounces evaporated milk, divided
1 package German chocolate cake mix with pudding
½ cup margarine, melted
1 cup chopped nuts
6 ounces chocolate chips

Preheat oven to 350°. In a saucepan over low heat, melt caramels with ⅓ cup evaporated milk. Combine remaining milk with cake mix, margarine, and nuts. Batter will be stiff.

Press half of cake mixture into a 9 x 13-inch pan and bake for 6 minutes. Sprinkle chocolate chips over crust. Add caramel mixture and spread to edges. Top with remaining cake mixture. Bake 15 to 20 minutes. Cool on rack, refrigerate. Cut into bars for serving.

Makes 4 dozen.

GERRY'S FAVORITE CHOCOLATE LUSH

Representative **Gerry Sikorski**—*Minnesota*

    1 cup flour
    2 teaspoons baking powder
    ½ teaspoon salt
    ¾ cup sugar
    2 tablespoons cocoa
    2 tablespoons oil
    ½ cup milk
    1 teaspoon vanilla
    ½ cup chopped nuts
    ¾ cup brown sugar
    2 tablespoons cocoa
    1¾ cups hot water

Combine first 5 dry ingredients. Add oil, milk, vanilla, and chopped nuts, mixing well. Spread onto ungreased 8 x 8 x 2-inch pan. Combine brown sugar, cocoa, and hot water. Pour over top of batter.

Bake in moderate oven at 350° for 45 minutes. Cut into squares. Top the inverted square with chocolate "lush" from bottom of the pan. Serve warm or cold with cream or ice cream.

Makes 9 servings.

Senator **Christopher Bond**—*Missouri*

This was named because my wife packed a container of these before we boarded a Governor's World Series Whistle-stop Train across Missouri on October 21, 1985. A friend from Greene County gets the credit for the brownie recipe and Governor Ashcroft earns applause for inviting us to join his family for the memorable journey. After boarding at Union Station in Kansas City, there were stops in Independence, Warrensburg, Sedalia, Jefferson City, Hermann, and Washington.

2 cups butter
8 squares unsweetened chocolate
8 eggs
4 cups sugar
pinch salt
1 teaspoon vanilla
2 cups flour, sifted
2 cups chopped nuts

Icing:
⅓ cup cocoa
⅓ cup butter
¼ milk
1 cup sugar
1 teaspoon vanilla

Preheat oven to 350°. Melt butter and chocolate over hot water in double boiler and set aside to cool. Beat eggs and add sugar, salt, and vanilla. Add cooled chocolate mixture. Fold in flour and chopped nuts. Pour into greased and floured 9 x 13-inch pan. Bake at 350° for 45 to 60 minutes over pan of hot water.

Combine all icing ingredients, except vanilla, and boil 3 minutes. Add vanilla and beat a few minutes. Pour icing over brownies. Cool and cut into 1½-inch squares.

Makes 6 dozen.

MRS. FASCELL'S
BUTTERSCOTCH BROWNIES

Representative **Dante Fascell**—*Florida*

14 ounces sweetened condensed milk
1 cup nuts
1½ cups graham cracker crumbs
6 ounces semisweet chocolate bits
6 ounces butterscotch bits

Mix all ingredients well and press into a well-buttered 9 x 9-inch baking dish. Bake for 30 minutes at 350°. Cut into small squares, but allow to cool in pan.

EASY GRAHAM CRACKER GOODIES

Representative **Carlos Moorhead**—*California*

graham crackers
¼ **cup butter**
¼ **pound margarine**
1 **cup brown sugar**
1 **cup pecans, chopped and toasted**

Grease cookie sheet with sides (jelly roll pan). Lay graham crackers on cookie sheet as close together as possible, covering entire sheet. In a saucepan, boil butter, margarine, and brown sugar for 2 minutes. Pour mixture over graham crackers and spread around to cover. Sprinkle with pecans. Let cool. Break up into pieces.

DREAM BARS

Senator **Alan Simpson**—*Wyoming*

A family favorite. We do not use the nuts for topping as it is very rich.

½ cup butter or margarine
1 cup flour

Filling:
2 eggs, well beaten
1½ cups brown sugar
2 tablespoons flour
½ teaspoon salt
¼ teaspoon baking powder
½ cup shredded coconut
1 cup walnuts, finely chopped

Topping:
2 tablespoons butter
1½ cups powdered sugar
2 tablespoons warm orange juice
1 tablespoon lemon juice
¼ cup chopped nuts, optional

Cream together butter and flour and spread in greased 8 x 8-inch pan. Bake 12 to 15 minutes at 325°, cool slightly.

For filling, beat eggs well. Add brown sugar, flour, salt, baking powder, nuts, and coconut. Spread over crust. Mix together topping ingredients except nuts and spread on top of filling. Bake 20 to 25 minutes at 325°. Top with nuts. Suitable for freezing.

LEMON BARS I

Senator **William Armstrong**—*Colorado*

½ cup butter
½ cup sugar
grated rind of ½ lemon
1¼ cups flour

Cream together butter, sugar, and lemon rind.
Gradually stir in flour. Press evenly over bottom of
13 x 9-inch pan. Bake in a preheated oven at 350°
until golden brown, about 15 minutes.

Filling:

2 eggs, slightly beaten
1 cup brown sugar, firmly packed
grated rind of ½ lemon
¼ cup flour
¼ teaspoon baking powder
1 cup walnuts, chopped

Beat eggs slightly. Add brown sugar, lemon rind,
flour, and baking powder. Beat to blend. Stir in
walnuts. Spread over hot, baked crust. Return to
oven to bake for 20 minutes longer. Place on wire
rack to cool.

Glaze:

1 cup powdered sugar
1 tablespoon butter, softened
2 tablespoons lemon juice

Blend above ingredients until smooth. While bars
are still warm, spread with glaze. Cool completely.

Makes 3 dozen bars.

LEMON BARS II

Representative **James Bilbray**—*Nevada*

> 1 cup butter
> 2 cups flour
> ½ teaspoon salt
> 1 cup powdered sugar
> 4 eggs
> 6 tablespoons lemon juice
> 6 tablespoons flour
> 1½ cups sugar

Mix butter, flour, salt, and powdered sugar in a large bowl. Pour into a cookie sheet that has sides to it. Bake for 20 minutes at 350°. Combine eggs, lemon juice, flour, and sugar. Beat well. Pour on top of previously baked mixture. Bake 25 minutes. When done, sprinkle with powdered sugar.

LEMON DAINTIES

Representative **Wes Watkins**—*Oklahoma*

Crust:
 1 cup butter
 ½ cup powdered sugar
 2 cups flour
 ½ teaspoon salt

Filling:
 4 eggs
 4 tablespoons flour
 2 cups sugar
 ¼ cup lemon juice

Grease bottom and sides of a 10 x 14-inch pan. Mix crust ingredients with pastry blender and press lightly into pan. Bake at 325° for 25 minutes, or until slightly brown.

While baking crust, mix together all filling ingredients with fork. Beat enough so that sugar is not grainy in texture. When crust is done, pour filling over hot crust. Bake another 25 minutes, or until slightly brown. Take from oven and top with sifted powdered sugar. Let cool and cut into squares to serve.

ORANGE OATMEAL ROUNDS

Representative **Jim Cooper**—*Tennessee*

This is our very favorite dessert.

½ cup shortening
1 cup brown sugar, packed
1 egg
2 tablespoons orange juice
1 tablespoon grated orange rind
1 cup rolled oats
½ cup raisins
1 cup flour, sifted
½ teaspoon soda
½ teaspoon salt
¼ cup coarsely chopped nuts

Cream shortening and sugar together. Add the egg and beat well. Mix in the orange juice and grated rind, rolled oats, and raisins. Sift together the flour, soda, and salt. Combine with the creamed mixture. Add nuts. Drop dough by teaspoonfuls onto greased baking sheets. Bake at 350° for 12 minutes.

Makes about 30 cookies.

SPECIAL K BARS

Representative **Byron Dorgan**—*North Dakota*

1 cup white sugar
1 cup light Karo syrup
¾ cup plain or crunchy peanut butter
5 to 6 cups Special K cereal
6 ounces butterscotch chips
6 ounces chocolate chips

Heat sugar and syrup on stove, stirring until mixture comes to a boil. Remove from stove and add peanut butter and Special K. Press mixture in a greased 8 x 8-inch pan. Melt butterscotch and chocolate chips together. Spread chip mixture over ingredients in pan. Cut into bars and serve.

GEB'S OATMEAL COOKIES

Representative **Beverly Byron**—*Maryland*

1½ cups flour
1 teaspoon baking soda
1 teaspoon salt
12 ounces chocolate chips
2 cups quick-cooking rolled oats
1 cup chopped nuts
1 cup butter
1 cup sugar
½ cup brown sugar
2 eggs
1 teaspoon vanilla

Mix together flour, baking soda, and salt. Add chocolate chips, rolled oats, and nuts. Cream together the butter, sugar, and brown sugar. Add eggs and vanilla. Blend all together well and drop by teaspoonfuls onto ungreased baking sheet. Bake at 350° for 12 minutes.

GRANDMOTHER MERRICK'S SOFT MOLASSES COOKIES

Senator **William Cohen**—*Maine*

⅓ cup shortening
½ cup boiling water
1 teaspoon salt
¾ cup molasses
½ cup granulated sugar
1 egg
2½ cups all-purpose flour, sifted
2 teaspoons baking powder
½ teaspoon baking soda
1 teaspoon ginger
1 teaspoon cinnamon

Place shortening in bowl. Pour in boiling water and add salt. Stir in molasses and sugar. Add unbeaten egg and beat well. Sift flour. Measure and sift it again together with baking powder, soda, ginger, and cinnamon. Stir into molasses mixture. Drop by spoonfuls onto greased cookie sheet. Bake at 375° for 12 to 15 minutes.

Makes 4 dozen cookies.

SPICY APPLE COOKIES

Senator **Chuck Grassley**—*Iowa*

½ cup shortening
1½ cups brown sugar
1 egg
2 cups flour
½ teaspoon cinnamon
¼ teaspoon nutmeg
½ teaspoon baking powder
½ teaspoon cloves
½ teaspoon baking soda
¼ cup milk
1 cup grated apple
1 cup raisins
½ cup nuts

Cream shortening, sugar, and egg. Sift dry ingredients and add alternately with milk. Add apple, raisins, and nuts. Bake in shallow baking sheet at 350° until done. Ice with your favorite vanilla frosting while hot.

LILLIAN'S BROWNIES

Representative **George Darden**—*Georgia*

Bar:
- ½ cup butter or margarine
- 1 ounce unsweetened chocolate
- 1 cup sugar
- 1 cup all-purpose flour
- 1 cup chopped nuts
- 1 teaspoon baking powder
- 1 teaspoon vanilla
- 2 eggs

Filling:
- 8 ounces cream cheese, softened (reserve 2 ounces for frosting)
- ½ cup sugar
- 2 tablespoons flour
- ¼ cup butter or margarine, softened
- 1 egg
- ½ teaspoon vanilla
- ¼ cup chopped nuts
- 6 ounces semisweet chocolate pieces, optional
- 3 cups miniature marshmallows

Frosting:
- ¼ cup butter or margarine
- 1 square (1 ounce) unsweetened chocolate remaining 2 ounces of cream cheese
- ¼ cup milk
- 1 pound (3 cups) powdered sugar
- 1 teaspoon vanilla

Preheat oven to 350°. Grease and flour 13 x 9-inch pan. In large saucepan, over low heat, melt butter and chocolate for bar. Add remaining bar ingredients. Mix well. Spread in prepared pan.

In a small bowl, combine cream cheese and next 5 filling ingredients. Blend until smooth and fluffy.

Stir in nuts. Spread over chocolate mixture. If desired, sprinkle with chocolate pieces. Bake for 25 to 30 minutes at 350° until toothpick inserted in center comes out clean. Sprinkle with marshmallows and bake 2 minutes longer.

In a large saucepan, over low heat, melt butter, chocolate, remaining cream cheese, and milk. Stir in powdered sugar and vanilla until smooth. Immediately pour over marshmallows and swirl together. Store in refrigerator.

Pies and Desserts

Pies

Cheesecakes

Tortes

Mousses

Puddings

SHOO-FLY PIE

Representative **Wes Watkins**—*Oklahoma*

This recipe came to Martha Watkins, daughter of the congressman, through her great-grandmother Rogers. It has been enjoyed by the family for at least four generations.

1 9-inch unbaked pastry shell
¼ cup sorghum
1 tablespoon water
¼ teaspoon soda
1½ cups flour, scant
1 cup brown sugar, firmly packed
¼ cup butter
¼ teaspoon soda

Cover bottom of unbaked pastry shell with sorghum. Mix in a little lukewarm water with finger. Mix in soda. Make crumbs of flour, brown sugar, butter, and soda. Cover sorghum mixture with crumb mixture. Bake at 350° for about 30 minutes.

SHOOFLY PIE

Representative **Robert Walker**—*Pennsylvania*

*Shoofly Pie is a traditional
Pennsylvania Dutch favorite.*

1 unbaked 9-inch pie crust
Crumb topping:
    1 cup flour
    ½ cup light brown sugar
    ¼ cup vegetable shortening
Liquid bottom:
    1 teaspoon baking soda
    1 cup boiling water
    1 cup golden table molasses
    ¼ teaspoon salt

Combine the flour, brown sugar, and shortening in a bowl. Cut with a pastry blender, or rub together, until fine crumbs are formed.

While preparing the liquid, put the unbaked pie shell in a preheated oven at 350° for about 5 minutes. This prevents the bottom from getting soggy.

In a bowl, dissolve the soda in the boiling water. Add the molasses and salt. Stir to blend well. Pour the liquid mixture into the prebaked pie shell. Sprinkle the crumb topping evenly on top. Bake at 375° for 10 minutes. Reduce the heat to 350° and bake for 30 minutes longer, until the center does not shake when it is moved.

Serve with whipped cream or ice cream, if desired. Freezes well!

Makes 6 servings.

Senator **Strom Thurmond**—*South Carolina*

This is my favorite dessert, and I hope that it can be used to help fight hunger.

3 **eggs**
1 **cup dark brown sugar**
1 **cup light corn syrup**
1 **tablespoon butter, melted**
⅛ **teaspoon salt**
1 **teaspoon vanilla**
1 **cup pecans, chopped**
1 **9-inch pastry shell**

Beat eggs, adding sugar gradually. Add syrup, butter, salt, vanilla, and pecans. Pour into a pastry shell and bake at 350° for 1 hour.

NO-CRUST PECAN PIE

Senator **Sam Nunn**—*Georgia*

> 3 large egg whites, room temperature
> 1 teaspoon baking powder
> 1 cup sugar
> 1 cup pecans, chopped
> 20 Ritz crackers, crushed
> 1 teaspoon vanilla
> ½ pint heavy cream, whipped

Beat egg whites until frothy. Add baking powder. Add sugar gradually, beating until stiff. Fold in pecans, crushed crackers, and vanilla. Pour into greased 8- or 9-inch pie pan. Bake at 300° for 40 minutes. Cool. Cover top with whipped cream.

May be prepared and refrigerated for 24 hours before serving.

Makes 6 to 8 servings.

PECAN PIE I

Representative **Lindy Boggs**—*Louisiana*

> 2 frozen pie crusts
> 3 eggs
> 1 cup sugar
> 1 cup light corn syrup
> 3 tablespoons melted butter
>   pinch of salt
> 1 teaspoon vanilla
>   pinch of each: cloves, nutmeg, cinnamon
> 2 cups shelled pecans

Take crusts from freezer while preparing other ingredients. When thawed, prick edges and bottom. Brush with butter.

Slightly beat eggs. Stir in sugar, syrup, butter, and pinch of salt. Beat. Add vanilla, cloves, nutmeg, and cinnamon. Gently stir in pecans. Place in pie shells. Bake at 350° for 40 to 50 minutes. The second pie can be frozen if you need only one.

Makes 12 to 16 servings, 2 pies.

PECAN PIE II

Representative **Lee Hamilton**—*Indiana*

One of the three kinds of pies requested each Thanksgiving by the Hamilton family members. The others are ususally blueberry and apple. The favorite way to eat them is a small slice of each and à. la mode for me.

½ **cup sugar**
¼ **cup margarine**
1 **cup light corn syrup**
¼ **teaspoon salt, optional**
3 **eggs**
1 **cup pecans (I like them whole)**

Cream sugar and margarine. Add syrup and salt. Beat well. Beat in eggs one at a time. Add pecans. Pour into a 9-inch pastry-lined pie pan. Bake at 350° for 1 hour and 10 minutes, or until knife comes out clean.

NO-BAKE BLUEBERRY PIE

Senator **Bob Packwood**—*Oregon*

⅓ cup melted margarine
1¼ cups graham cracker crumbs
3 tablespoons sugar
1 box fresh blueberries
10 ounces red currant jelly
   sour cream

Melt margarine in saucepan, adding graham cracker crumbs and sugar. Press into a 9-inch pie pan. Bake at 350° for 8 minutes. Cool. Fill crust with blueberries (it may not take all of them). Drizzle room-temperature jelly over top of berries. Cover with thick layer of sour cream. Chill overnight.

HUCKLEBERRY PIE

Senator **Max Baucus**—*Montana*

1   9-inch unbaked pie shell
½   cup sugar or honey
1   pint fresh huckleberries
1   tablespoon flour
     butter

Mix sugar, huckleberries, and flour together. Place in pie shell and dot liberally with butter. Bake for 30 to 40 minutes at 350°.

The "secret" of this recipe is the special berries which can only come from the mountainous elevations, chiefly in the West. The taste comes with the eating, but even more so if the person who makes the pie was in on the collection of the berries. They grow with abandon on green wooded slopes just under the treeline and may be accessible only on dirt roads (put there by timber companies of the U.S. Forest Service), preferably on sunny days in late July and early August. The choice spots vary each year, which means that pickers have elaborate games in store either to include or exclude fellow pickers from their favorite slopes. Some people who would entertain a crowd with the results of the day's foray would never dream of revealing the lush and abundant grounds they trod in pursuit of their elusive prize. For these berries—which New Englanders are apt to call blueberries, although the two species do not taste the same to all connoisseurs—are shamelessly shy and do not readily reveal themselves to heavyfooted and acquisitive souls. They require some shade and moisture, and intermittent sun before they develop their large, smooth, glistening roundness. So splendid and rare a taste they are that black, brown, even grizzly bears also treasure them and a person may run interference with one or more of these massive creatures when the season is at its height. The higher the elevation, the more likely the bears. So the picker dresses wisely, and watches well. He or she may add a tiny bell to his picking can (plastic buckets are best, with large handles) and so warn off the competitors. The bears need to fill up their stomachs in preparation for the long winter's hibernation ahead. The anxious pie-lover (or jelly or jam maker, or syrup lover, or any of a number of combinations of these types) only stalks the lonely forests at his peril; but that also gives some added piquancy to the chase. Picking is handwork, unless you fall into the school that appreciates modern marvels and may then choose a carefully crafted wooden box with a claw-like aperture that can swoop through the berry bushes and haphazardly collect bunches that fall back into the receptacle below. But you are apt to collect just as many of the bitter green leaves as well.

Wardrobe is important, too, and the company one chooses. Always include a foul-weather slicker, in a bright color (those bears again—they are shy, too, and might back off if a yellow or red human being is on the trail), and a rainhat and heavy boots for climbing. Part of the fun is hiking with friends, picnicking in a lovely glen. Part of it is exercise—stopping constantly, and talking or singing as you go. The rest of the fun is in filling the buckets and then dumping each one into the larger group pot at some central location, then, at the end of the afternoon, carrying home the precious and painfully acquired berries to be divided up among all—and eventually into pies. Best of all is baking one immediately, for a sort of instant reward, although the berries can be put into tiny plastic bags and stored in the refrigerator, even the freezer. (They can be a very liquid mass after thawing.)

This guarantees that a good pie is a good memory, and not just another meal.

LEMONADE PIE

Senator **Chuck Grassley**—*Iowa*

Guaranteed to get 'em home for dinner—even a congressman!

6 **ounces frozen lemonade**
14 **ounces sweetened condensed milk**
4 **ounces Cool Whip**
1 **9-inch graham cracker crust**

Thaw lemonade. Mix lemonade and milk. Fold into Cool Whip. Place in a graham cracker crust. Chill. If desired, top with cherry or blueberry pie filling.

SWISH PIE

Senator **Chuck Grassley**—*Iowa*

This is oh, so good.

14 ounces sweetened condensed milk
¼ cup lemon juice
½ cup nuts, chopped
20 ounces crushed pineapple, with juice
8 ounces Cool Whip
1 9-inch graham cracker crust

Mix milk and lemon juice. Add all other ingredients and place in graham cracker crust. Chill.

LEMON MERINGUE PIE

Senator **Rudy Boschwitz**—*Minnesota*

  1 8-inch crumb or baked pastry shell, chilled
  ½ cup lemon juice
  1 teaspoon grated lemon rind, or ¼ teaspoon
     lemon extract
14 ounces sweetened condensed milk
  2 eggs, separated
  ¼ teaspoon cream of tartar
  4 tablespoons sugar

Combine lemon juice and grated lemon rind.
Gradually stir into condensed milk. Add egg yolks
and stir until well blended. Pour into chilled crust.
Add cream of tartar to egg whites. Blend until
almost stiff enough to hold peaks. Add sugar
gradually (one tablespoon at a time) until stiff but
not dry. Pile meringue lightly on pie filling. Bake in
slow oven (325°) until lightly browned, about 15
minutes. Cool.

MAPLE APPLE PIE

Senator **James Jeffords**—*Vermont*

*Here is an old and typical
Vermont recipe.*

1 **9-inch pie crust, unbaked**
4 **apples**
½ **cup maple sugar**
2 **tablespoons butter
  cinnamon (optional)**
⅔ **cup cream**

Pare and core apples, cut in quarters. Arrange on pie crust. Sprinkle generously with maple sugar and dot with butter. Cinnamon may be added to taste. Pour cream over apple mixture. Bake at 450° for 10 minutes. Reduce to 350° and bake until the apples are soft.

CRUMB TOPPING APPLE PIE

Senator **Paul Simon**—*Illinois*

From the kitchen of Evelyn Knop, mother-in-law of Sheila Simon, and now a Simon family favorite.

1 **9-inch pie shell, unbaked**
4 **cups apples, peeled and diced**
½ **cup sugar**
¼ **teaspoon cinnamon**
⅛ **teaspoon nutmeg**
½ **tablespoon butter**
¼ **cup margarine**
1 **cup flour**
¾ **cup brown sugar**

Place apples in unbaked pie shell. Sprinkle with sugar, cinnamon, and nutmeg. Dot with butter. For topping, melt margarine and add flour and brown sugar. Mix until crumbled and sprinkle over the apples. Bake at 350° for 35 to 40 minutes.

CAROL'S BUTTER CRUST

Senator **Chuck Grassley**—*Iowa*

½ **cup melted butter**
1 **cup flour**
1 **tablespoon sugar**

Mix ingredients together in pie plate. Press out. Bake until brown, 10 to 12 minutes at 350°.

SAM'S SCRUMPTIOUS PIE

Senator **Christopher Bond**—*Missouri*

Guaranteed to be a hit with the preschool set and their parents. Combining all Sam's favorite things, this frozen delight is not for weight watchers.

Graham cracker crust:
    2⅓ **cups cinnamon graham cracker crumbs**
    ¾ **cup butter, melted**
    ⅓ **cup granulated sugar**
    ⅔ **cup cocoa powder, sifted**
Ice cream filling:
    2¾ **pints vanilla ice cream**
    ½ **cup peanut butter**
    ½ **cup semisweet chocolate chips**
Chocolate sauce:
    2 **ounces unsweetened chocolate**
    3 **tablespoons butter**
    1 **cup sugar**
    1 **rounded tablespoon flour**
    1 **cup cold water**
    1 **teaspoon vanilla**

Mix together crumbs, butter, sugar, and cocoa until well combined. Press firmly into a 10-inch pie plate to make solid bottom crust. Freeze until ready to use.

By hand, combine ice cream with peanut butter and chocolate chips. Spoon into crust. Freeze immediately until solid, about 2 hours or overnight. Top each serving with chocolate sauce.

Note: Do not let ice cream get too soft before mixing with peanut butter.

In saucepan, melt chocolate and butter over low heat. Mix sugar and flour, add to chocolate mixture. Add water. Cook over medium heat, stirring constantly until thick. Add vanilla, beat until smooth.

Makes 8 servings.

CHIPPED CHOCOLATE PIE

Senator **Orrin Hatch**—*Utah*

      35 large marshmallows
      ½ cup milk
       2 squares bitter or unsweetened chocolate,
         chipped
      ½ pint whipped whipping cream, or 1 small
         container Cool Whip
       1 10-inch graham cracker crust
         chopped nuts, cherries, or chipped
         sweetened chocolate

Melt marshmallows with milk in double boiler or
microwave. Cool. Beat well. Fold in 2 squares of
chipped bitter or unsweetened chocolate and ½ pint
of whipped whipping cream. Pour into graham
cracker crust. Top with chopped nuts, cherries, or
chipped chocolate, as desired. Chill in refrigerator
for at least 2 hours.

CHOCOLATE CHIP PIE

Representative **Steve Gunderson**—*Wisconsin*

½ cup milk
18 large marshmallows
½ pint whipping cream
2 squares semisweet chocolate (grated)
1 9-inch graham cracker pie crust

Heat milk in double boiler, add marshmallows and stir until smooth (can be melted in microwave). Cool. Whip whipping cream and add grated chocolate to it. Add whipped cream mixture to cooled marshmallow mixture. Pour into graham cracker crust. Serve chilled. For a 9 x 13-inch cake pan, double the recipe.

A holiday meal at the Gundersons' would not be right without my mother's chocolate chip pie. It's a family tradition. With three sisters, four brothers, their spouses, nieces and nephews, it's good that this is an easy recipe to double!

SONNY'S FAVORITE CHOCOLATE PIE

Representative **G. V. Montgomery**—*Mississippi*

1¼ cups sugar
1 tablespoon cornstarch
¼ teaspoon salt
3 tablespoons flour
4 tablespoons cocoa
4 eggs, separated
2½ cups milk
1 tablespoon margarine
1 teaspoon vanilla
7 tablespoons sugar
¼ teaspoon cream of tartar
1 9-inch baked pie shell

Mix first 5 ingredients and add beaten egg yolks and milk. With a mixer, beat until lumps dissolve. Cook over low heat, stirring constantly until thick. Remove from heat and mix in margarine and vanilla. Pour into baked pie shell. Whip egg whites until frothy and stiff. Stir cream of tartar into the sugar. Add to the egg whites 1 tablespoon at a time while beating. Pour over pie filling and bake at 350° until lightly browned.

PUMPKIN CHEESE CAKE

Senator **John C. Danforth**—*Missouri*

32 ounces cream cheese, softened
1½ cups sugar
5 large eggs
16 ounces canned pumpkin
¼ cup flour
1 teaspoon cinnamon
1 teaspoon nutmeg
pinch of ginger
pinch of salt
whipped topping

Beat cheese until fluffy and gradually add sugar. Beat in eggs one at a time. Add remaining ingredients except whipped topping. Pour mixture into greased, 10-inch springform pan. Bake at 325° for 90 minutes. Turn oven off and let set for 30 minutes. Serve with whipped topping. May be frozen.

Makes 10 to 12 servings.

CHEESECAKE EXTRAORDINAIRE

Representative **Mary Rose Oakar**—*Ohio*

If you notice, this cheesecake is made in one mixing bowl and is really very easy to prepare.

16 ounces soft cream cheese
1 pound creamed cottage cheese
1½ cups sugar
4 eggs, slightly beaten
3 tablespoons cornstarch
3 tablespoons flour
1½ teaspoons lemon juice
1 teaspoon vanilla
½ cup butter or margarine, melted
1 pint dairy sour cream
   fresh strawberries, blueberries, or pineapple

Preheat oven to 325°. Grease a 10-inch springform pan. In large bowl of an electric mixer, at high speed, beat cream cheese with cottage cheese until creamy. Gradually beat in sugar, then beat in eggs until well combined. At low speed, beat in cornstarch, flour, lemon juice, and vanilla. Add melted butter and sour cream. Beat just until smooth.

Pour into prepared pan, bake 1 hour and 10 minutes, or until firm around the edges. Turn off oven. Let cake stand in oven 2 hours. Remove cake from oven, let cool completely. Refrigerate until well chilled—several hours. To serve, run spatula around side of cheesecake to loosen from pan. Remove side of springform pan and leave bottom of pan in place. Serve with fresh berries.

Makes 12 servings.

PUMPKIN TORTE

Senator **Charles Grassley**—*Iowa*

Clipped from a farm magazine, and it's delicious. One of my very favorites.

Crust:
- 24 graham crackers, crushed
- ⅓ cup sugar
- ½ cup butter

First layer:
- 2 eggs, beaten
- ¾ cup sugar
- 8 ounces cream cheese

Second layer:
- 2 cups pumpkin
- 3 egg yolks
- ½ cup sugar
- ½ cup milk
- ½ teaspoon salt
- 1 tablespoon cinnamon
- 1 envelope plain gelatin
- ¼ cup cold water
- 3 egg whites
- ¼ cup sugar

Mix crust ingredients and press into 9 x 13-inch pan. Mix first layer and pour over crust. Bake for 20 minutes at 350°. Cool.

Meanwhile, cook pumpkin, egg yolks, ½ cup sugar, milk, salt, and cinnamon until mixture thickens. Remove from heat and add gelatin which has been dissolved in cold water. Cool. Beat egg whites and ¼ cup sugar, then fold into cooled pumpkin mixture. Pour over cooled, baked crust. Refrigerate and serve with whipped cream.

APPLE CRISP

Representative **Fred Grandy**—*Iowa*

4 cups apples
1 teaspoon cinnamon
1 teaspoon nutmeg
1 tablespoon lemon juice
½ cup water
1 cup sugar
¾ cup flour
½ cup margarine, softened

Peel and slice apples. Coat a square, 9-inch cake pan with spray shortening. Place apple slices in it and sprinkle with cinnamon and nutmeg. Add lemon juice and water. Mix sugar, flour, and margarine until the combination crumbles. Spread this over the fruit. Bake uncovered for 1 hour at 350°. Serve with vanilla ice cream.

APPLE CRUMBLE

Senator **Paul Sarbanes**—*Maryland*

This is our family's favorite dessert and comes from England.

1½ **pounds large cooking apples**
4 **tablespoons sugar**
juice of half a lemon
¼ **teaspoon cinnamon**
¼ **pound butter**
2 **cups flour**
½ **cup sugar**
¼ **teaspoon ground ginger**

Peel apples, then core and cut into eighths. Mix in a 1-quart baking dish with sugar, lemon juice, and cinnamon. In a mixing bowl, put in butter and flour. Rub butter into the flour until it is the consistency of fine bread crumbs. Add sugar and ginger and mix in well. Sprinkle the crumble over the apples and press down lightly.

Bake at 350° until golden brown and apples are cooked, 30 to 40 minutes. Serve with small jug of thick cream, unwhipped. This is also good made with other fruit—blueberries, peaches, etc.

PEACH COBBLER

Representative **George Darden**—*Georgia*

½ cup margarine
1½ cups sugar, divided
¾ cup flour
1½ teaspoons baking powder
1 teaspoon salt
¾ cup milk
1 tablespoon lemon juice
3 cups sliced peaches

Preheat oven to 350°. Melt margarine in a 9 x 11-inch pan in preheating oven. In mixing bowl combine ¾ cup sugar, flour, baking powder, and salt. Stir in the milk, blending well.

Add the remaining ¾ cup sugar and the lemon juice to the fruit. Place the fruit evenly in the pan over the melted margarine. Pour the batter mixture over the fruit but do not stir in. Bake at 350° for 30 minutes. May be served plain or top each serving with vanilla ice cream.

Makes 6 to 8 servings.

CARAMEL DUMPLINGS

Representative **Timothy Penny**—*Minnesota*

Syrup:
- 1 cup brown sugar
- ½ cup water
- 2 tablespoons butter

Dumplings:
- ¼ cup sugar
- 1 egg
- 2 tablespoons butter
- ½ cup milk
- ½ teaspoon vanilla
- 1¾ cups flour
- 2 teaspoons baking powder
- ¼ teaspoon salt

Mix syrup ingredients together and boil for 2 minutes. Pour into a 9 x 13-inch pan. Mix together dumpling ingredients and drop by spoonfuls into syrup. Bake at 350° for 20 minutes.

BAKLAVA

Representative **Olympia Snowe**—*Maine*

    1 **pound butter**
    1 **pound phyllo dough (strudel leaves)**
 1½ **pounds walnuts, chopped**
   ¾ **cup sugar**
    1 **teaspoon cinnamon**
      grated rind of 1 orange
Syrup:
    2 **cups water**
    2 **cups sugar**
   ½ **cup honey**
    1 **cinnamon stick**
    3 **lemon slices**

Melt butter and brush on a 13 x 9-inch pan. Place 1 layer of phyllo in pan allowing ends to extend over pan. Brush with melted butter. Repeat with 4 sheets of phyllo.

Mix nuts, sugar, cinnamon, and orange rind. Sprinkle phyllo heavily with nut mixture. Continue to alternate 1 layer of phyllo, brush with melted butter, then sprinkle heavily with nut mixture until all ingredients are used. Be sure to reserve 4 sheets of phyllo for the top (each to be brushed with butter).

Brush top with remaining butter, trim edges with sharp knife. Cut through top with diagonal lines to form diamond shapes. Bake at 400° for 15 minutes. Lower oven to 300° and continue to bake for 40 minutes. Should be golden brown in color.

To make syrup: cook first 4 syrup ingredients over medium heat on stove until thick. Add lemon slices. Cook 3 minutes. Remove cinnamon and lemon.

While pastry is still hot, cover with prepared syrup
and let stand overnight before serving. Baklava
should rest for 24 hours before removing from pan.
Will keep in refrigerator for weeks or can be frozen.

Makes 23 servings.

MAINE BLUEBERRY
JELLO DESSERT

Senator **George Mitchell**—*Maine*

This is also a great summer salad.

2 small packages grape gelatin
#2 can (20 ounces) crushed pineapple, drained, reserving juice
1 can Maine Blueberry Pie Filling Mix
8 ounces softened cream cheese
½ pint sour cream
½ cup sugar
1 teaspoon vanilla
chopped pecans or walnuts

Add 1 cup boiling water to gelatin, and the juice from the pineapple plus enough boiling water to make 1 cup (total 2 cups liquid). Add pineapple and blueberry mix. Spread in a 9 x 13-inch Pyrex dish and chill until it is set. Combine cream cheese, sour cream, sugar, and vanilla. Spread over chilled gelatin. Sprinkle chopped walnuts on top and serve.

FROSTY STRAWBERRY SQUARES

Representative **Joel Hefley**—*Colorado*

> 1 cup flour, sifted
> ¼ cup brown sugar
> ½ cup walnuts or pecans, chopped
> ½ cup butter or margarine
> 2 egg whites
> 1 cup granulated sugar
> 2 cups fresh strawberries, sliced, or 10-ounce package frozen berries partially thawed
> 2 tablespoons lemon juice
> 1 cup heavy cream, whipped
> strawberries for garnish

Mix flour, brown sugar, walnuts, and butter with a pastry cutter. Spread in a shallow baking pan. Bake at 350° for 20 minutes, stirring several times to keep mixture crumbly. Spread ⅔ of crumbled mixture in a 9 x 13-inch baking pan.

Combine egg whites, sugar, berries, and lemon juice and beat on high speed with electric mixer until stiff peaks form. Fold in whipped cream. Spread over crumbs. Top with remaining crumbs. Freeze at least 6 hours. Garnish with fresh strawberries.

Makes 12 servings.

STRAWBERRY ICE CREAM

Senator **Harry Reid**—*Nevada*

2 **pints strawberries**
1 **cup sugar**
  vanilla
1 **cup heavy cream**
2 **cups half-and-half**

Puree strawberries in food processor or blender. Add sugar and a little vanilla. Add cream and half-and-half. Freeze mixture in ice-cream maker. Serve.

LEMON MOUSSE

Senator **Christopher Bond**—*Missouri*

This refreshing and simple-to-prepare mousse is equally appealing when served over fresh blueberries, raspberries, blackberries, or strawberries. Prepare enough for seconds.

5 **eggs, separated**
1 **cup sugar, divided**
  juice of 2 large lemons
1 **cup heavy cream, whipped**
2 **teaspoons grated lemon rind**
1 **quart berries**

In a nonaluminum double boiler, beat egg yolks and ¾ cup of sugar until mixture becomes thick and lemon-colored. Add lemon juice. Cook over simmering water, stirring constantly, until mixture heavily coats the spoon. Caution: Do not allow to boil. Remove from heat, cool. Beat egg whites until stiff, fold into lemon mixture. Fold in whipped cream and lemon rind until mousse is smooth. Chill. Pour berries into a glass serving bowl, sprinkle with remaining sugar. Just before serving, cover berries with mousse.

Makes 8 servings.

ENGLISH CREAM DESSERT

Senator **Bob Packwood**—*Oregon*

Raspberries are great with this dessert. It is ironic that a cookbook could be used to fight hunger!

1 **pint heavy sweet cream**
1 **cup granulated sugar**
1 **packet unflavored gelatin**
1 **pint sour cream**
1 **tablespoon vanilla (optional)**

Heat heavy cream, but do not boil. Add sugar and mix until dissolved. Add gelatin and dissolve. Remove mixture from heat and add it to sour cream. Stir in vanilla if desired. Beat until smooth. Pour into serving dish or mold and refrigerate at least 4 hours. Serve with fruit.

BROWNIE PUDDING

Representative **Bill Richardson**—*New Mexico*

⅓ cup sugar
1 teaspoon baking powder
½ cup flour
3 tablespoons unsweetened cocoa
¼ cup milk
1 tablespoon melted butter
1 teaspoon vanilla
¼ cup walnuts, chopped
½ cup brown sugar, packed
¾ cup boiling water
whipped cream

Sift together sugar, baking powder, flour, and 1 tablespoon cocoa. Add milk, butter, vanilla, and walnuts. Mix thoroughly. Spread in well-greased, square casserole dish. Combine brown sugar, remaining cocoa, and boiling water. Pour over mixture in baking dish. Bake at 350° for 35 to 40 minutes. Cool slightly. Serve with whipped cream. May be frozen.

Makes 6 servings.

GRANDMA'S CHRISTMAS PUDDING

Senator **James McClure**—*Idaho*

2¾ cups flour
1 teaspoon baking soda
1 teaspoon salt
1 teaspoon cinnamon
1 teaspoon nutmeg
¼ teaspoon allspice
¼ teaspoon ground cloves
½ cup sugar
1 cup coarsely ground suet (tender leaf part)
1 cup nuts, finely chopped
½ cup raisins
½ cup molasses
½ cup dark Karo syrup
1 cup hot water

Sauce:
2 cups water
2 tablespoons butter
¼ teaspoon salt
1 cup sugar
½ cup flour, scant
½ teaspoon nutmeg
½ teaspoon vanilla

Topping:
whipped cream

Sift dry ingredients together and sprinkle some over the suet, nuts, and raisins. Mix, coating them to prevent them from sticking together. Mix remaining dry ingredients with the liquids. Stir in suet mixture. Pour into a greased and sugared 8-cup pudding mold. Set the tightly covered mold on a trivet in an inch of boiling water in a heavy kettle. Cover kettle closely and turn the heat on high. As steam begins to escape, lower the heat. Steam for 3 hours, adding more boiling water to the kettle as needed.

When it is done, remove lid and let stand awhile before unmolding. Serve with hot sauce and top with whipped cream.

For sauce, boil together the water, butter, and salt. Mix sugar and flour and add to boiled mixture. Add nutmeg and vanilla. Stir until thickened.

Makes 18 servings.

MOM HARDMAN'S PERSIMMON PUDDING

Representative **John T. Myers**—*Indiana*

Wild persimmons are native to the Seventh District of Indiana and Mom Hardman made the best use of them! You'll find persimmon pudding being sold every fall at practically every festival in my district.

1 **quart whole persimmons**
1 **quart milk**
2½ **cups flour**
2 **cups sugar**
½ **teaspoon baking soda**
   pinch salt
1 **heaping teaspoon baking powder**
1 **teaspoon cinnamon**
1 **egg, beaten**
⅓ **stick butter, melted**

Press persimmons and milk through a strainer together. Add flour, sugar, baking soda, salt, baking powder, and cinnamon to persimmon-milk mixture. Add egg and butter. Put pudding in a 9 x 13-inch baking pan. Bake 1½ to 2 hours at 350° or until dark brown.

NATILLAS

Senator **Pete Domenici**—*New Mexico*

This is a favorite New Mexico dessert.

4 **eggs, separated**
¼ **cup flour**
1 **quart whole milk**
¾ **cup sugar**
⅛ **teaspoon salt**
dash nutmeg

Make paste of egg yolks, flour, and 1 cup milk. Add sugar and salt to remaining milk and scald at medium temperature. Add egg mixture to scalded milk and continue to cook at medium temperature until it reaches consistency of soft custard. Remove from heat and cool to room temperature. Beat egg whites until stiff, but not dry, and fold into the custard. Chill well before serving. Spoon into individual dishes. Sprinkle with nutmeg and serve.

Makes 6 to 8 servings.

BANANAS FOSTER

Representative **Chalmers P. Wylie**—*Ohio*

¾ **cup butter or margarine**
2 **cups brown sugar**
2 **ounces white rum**
2 **ounces banana liqueur**
6 **bananas, peeled and cut lengthwise**
vanilla ice cream
cinnamon

Melt butter or margarine over low heat. Add brown sugar and stir until melted. Add rum and banana liqueur. Cook and stir approximately 2 minutes. Add bananas. Cook until bananas are heated, approximately 2 minutes. Serve over vanilla ice cream. Top with cinnamon.

Makes 6 to 8 servings.

SUGAR COOKIE PIZZA

Senator **Ernest Hollings**—*South Carolina*

1 20-ounce roll refrigerated sugar cookie
   dough, room temperature
12 ounces cream cheese, softened
¼ cup sugar
1 tablespoon lemon juice
   grated rind of 1 lemon
3 fresh fruits (strawberries, blueberries,
   pineapple, or banana)
3 tablespoons marmalade (orange, apricot,
   or peach)
2 tablespoons Kirsch

Press cookie dough onto a well-greased pizza pan.
Bake at 375° for 14 to 16 minutes. Cool. Combine
next 4 ingredients in a food processor. Spread over
crust. Arrange fruit in pleasing pattern. Combine
and heat marmalade and Kirsch. Brush over top of
fruit. Chill before serving.

Makes 8 servings.

Potpourri

Snacks

Sauces

Drinks

IDAHO HONEY-BAKED APPLES

Senator **Steve Symms**—*Idaho*

Here's a simple to fix recipe that combines all-natural ingredients—especially Idaho apples and honey—into a delicious breakfast treat or dessert for family or friends. The taste is unique, and the appearance is festive.

6 **large Rome apples**
6 **tablespoons Idaho honey**
¼ **cup orange juice**
2 **tablespoons sugar**
1 **teaspoon nutmeg**
1 **orange**

Core apples, being careful not to cut all the way through. Peel about ⅓ of the way down from stem end. Combine honey and orange juice. Pour into centers of apples. Set in a baking dish. Pour a little hot water in bottom of the pan. Bake at 400° for 50 to 60 minutes, or until apples are tender. Sprinkle tops with a little sugar and nutmeg. Run under broiler to glaze. Quarter orange slices and tuck them in center of apples after glazing.

Makes 6 servings.

ICING

Senator **Chuck Grassley**—*Iowa*

From Agnes, who can really bake.

1 tablespoon butter
2 cups powdered sugar
⅛ teaspoon salt
½ teaspoon vanilla
3 tablespoons milk

Mix together and ice cookies or cakes.

CRANBERRY-APPLE-PEAR SAUCE

Senator **Christopher Bond**—*Missouri*

Always included with our Thanksgiving turkey, this festive combination of fruits draws accolades when teamed with a wheel of brie on a holiday buffet table at Christmas.

2 **pounds fresh cranberries**
4 **apples—pared, cored, and diced**
3 **pears—pared, cored, and diced**
2 **cups golden raisins**
2 **cups sugar**
1 **cup fresh orange juice**
2½ **tablespoons grated orange rind**
2 **teaspoons cinnamon**
¼ **teaspoon freshly grated nutmeg**
½ **cup plus 2 tablespoons orange-flavored liqueur**

Place all ingredients, except liqueur, in a large saucepan. Bring to a boil, reduce heat. Simmer uncovered 45 minutes, stirring frequently until mixture thickens. Remove from heat. Stir in liqueur, cool. Refrigerate at least 4 hours. Serve sauce slightly chilled with pork, chicken, or turkey.

Makes 6 cups.

HOT MULLED CIDER

Representative **Wes Watkins**—*Oklahoma*

If you have a lime build-up in your percolator, this will delime it. So run vinegar or a deliming agent through first if necessary.

46 **ounces apple juice or cider**
3 **rounded tablespoons brown sugar**
2 **rounded tablespoons red-hots**
2 **sticks cinnamon, broken**
1 **teaspoon whole cloves**
1 **teaspoon whole allspice**

Pour juice into 9–12-cup percolator. Fit filter into coffee well. Into filter put brown sugar, red-hots, and spices. Perk as you would coffee. Delicious!

Makes 6 servings.

PUNCH

Representative **Wes Watkins**—*Oklahoma*

This is a refreshing punch and won't stain carpets!

4 **packages unsweetened Kool-Aid**
4 **cups sugar**
4 **quarts water**
1 **can pineapple juice**
　Sprite or Seven-Up soda pop

Mix Kool-Aid, sugar, water, and pineapple juice in container. Stir until sugar is dissolved. It dissolves well if hot water is used with first quart. Freeze at least 2 days.

Set out to thaw no less than 2 hours before you are to serve it. As it thaws, carve on the frozen part to help it get slushy. Fill punch bowl halfway with punch slush and add Sprite or Seven-Up to fill bowl. If any is left and you want to refreeze it, let it completely thaw. It won't refreeze right if ice crystals are on it when refreezing starts.

SCHROEDER BREAKFAST

Representative **Pat Schroeder**—*Colorado*

Instructions for preparation:
1. Find a bowl. If on the floor, wash it because the dog probably was using it.
2. Locate a box of cereal—preferably sugar-coated, then a search for the sugar won't be necessary.
3. Get milk from the refrigerator, but be sure and check the spoil date on it.
4. Find a spoon. Again, if on the floor, wash it.
5. Put cereal in bowl, add milk, and insert spoon.
6. Eat.
7. Rinse dirty dishes and place in the dishwasher. Opening the dishwasher will not make you sterile.

CRANBERRY-TANGERINE CHUTNEY

Representative **James Sensenbrenner**—*Wisconsin*

4 tangerines
2 cups fresh cranberries
1 apple, peeled and diced
½ cup vinegar
½ cup orange marmalade
½ cup golden raisins
1½ cups water
1¼ cups sugar
1 tablespoon curry powder
¾ teaspoon cinnamon
½ teaspoon ginger
¼ teaspoon ground cloves
dash allspice

Peel tangerines and remove all seeds and membranes. Cut sections in half. Combine all ingredients in saucepan and bring to boil over medium heat. Reduce heat and cover. Simmer for 30 to 40 minutes, stirring occasionally. Store in hot, sterilized, sealed jars or in covered container in refrigerator.

Makes about 8 cups.

CORN DODGERS

Representative **Porter Goss**—*Florida*

> 1 cup white corn meal
> 1 teaspoon salt
> 2 cups boiling water
> 1 tablespoon Crisco

Add corn meal and salt to boiling water. Cook a few minutes until quite thick. Thin with milk. Make into a "pone" (oval shape). Have heavy skillet greased with Crisco or bacon fat. Bake in oven until brown.

WINE SAUCE FOR LAMB

Representative **Porter Goss**—*Florida*

    1 cup currant jelly
    1 cup wine
    1 cup brandy
    ¾ cup brown sugar
    1 cup catsup
    ½ pint lamb gravy/juice (after grease is removed)
    cloves or allspice to taste

Heat all ingredients in a double boiler. Thicken with a little flour. Serve over lamb.

INDEX BY RECIPE

INDEX BY CONTRIBUTOR

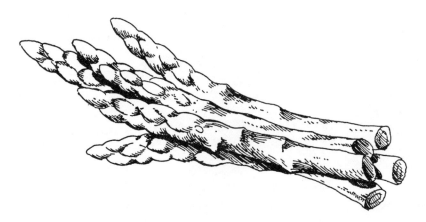

INDEX BY STATE

THE NEW AMERICAN SAMPLER COOKBOOK

was composed in 11/13 Palatino on a Varityper system
by Professional Book Compositors, Inc.;
printed by web offset on 55-pound, acid free,
Glatfelter B-16 Natural stock,
Smyth sewn and bound over .098" binders' boards
in Holliston Roxite cloth, with 80-pound Rainbow endpapers,
and wrapped with dust jackets printed in four colors
on 80-pound enamel stock and film laminated
by Arcata Graphics Book Group / Hawkins;
designed by Will Underwood;
and published by
THE KENT STATE UNIVERSITY PRESS
Kent, Ohio 44242